INNOVATION WITH PURPOSE

LOCKHEED MARTIN'S FIRST 100 YEARS

LOCKHEED MARTIN

100 YEARS OF
ACCELERATING
TOMORROW

First Edition
ISBN 9781882771394
Library of Congress Control Number 2013944744

Produced by The History Factory
1919 M Street Northwest, Suite 610
Washington, D.C. 20036
www.historyfactory.com

Published by Lockheed Martin Corporation
6801 Rockledge Drive
Bethesda, MD 20817
www.lockheedmartin.com

TABLE OF CONTENTS

FOREWORD

"THERE HAS NEVER BEEN A SENSATION MORE
SOUL-SATISFYING THAN THE FIRST FLIGHT OF A NEW
DESIGN; NO FIELD OF ENDEAVOR HALF SO FASCINATING
AS THE CHALLENGE OF EACH NEW SECRET OF FLIGHT."

—GLENN L. MARTIN

"FLYING HAS NO BARRIERS."

—ALLAN LOCKHEED

With those words, Allan Lockheed and Glenn Martin captured the spirit of what it means to be a Lockheed Martin employee. We are driven by achievement. We live to take on the obstacles that others deem impossible, and rise to the challenges of today and tomorrow.

If innovation is our company's beating heart, purpose is our soul. We're at our best when we're working to make the world a better place through technology.

Talk to Lockheed Martin employees, and they'll tell you they're not just building airplanes, radars and missile defense systems — they're helping U.S. and allied forces strengthen global security. They're not just writing software — they're helping governments deliver essential services to millions of citizens. They're not just designing satellites and rockets — they're expanding the boundaries of scientific discovery.

Throughout these pages, you'll find hundreds of examples of innovation with purpose. From pioneering a new industry at the dawn of aviation, to powering the arsenal of democracy in World War II, to delivering the cutting-edge technology that helped win the Cold War, we're proud to have made an enduring contribution to history. Looking ahead to our next 100 years, we're honored to do our part to shape the future.

This book is dedicated to the hundreds of thousands of men and women who have been a part of Lockheed Martin and its heritage companies over the past century. You know firsthand just how soul-satisfying innovation with purpose can be. These stories are a tribute to the role you've played in writing the amazing story of our history and creating the unlimited horizons of our future.

Marillyn A. Hewson
Chief Executive Officer and President
July 2013

CHAPTER 1

WORKSHOPS

The Dawn of an Industry

1886-1926

"I DON'T SEE THE SENSE OF THROWING AWAY ALL YOU'VE GOT BY MESSING AROUND WITH THOSE FLYING MACHINES."[1]

—CLARENCE MARTIN,
FATHER OF MARTIN COMPANY FOUNDER GLENN MARTIN

IN THE GARAGE, ON THE WING

Spruce. Bamboo. Cotton. Glue. These were the high-tech materials of 1909, the tools of a tinkerer. At the end of each day, 23-year-old Glenn Luther Martin closed up his motorcar dealership and lugged these raw materials to a rented Methodist church a block and a half away. The sacred space served as an incubator for one of the century's most innovative companies and a fitting workshop for the creation of man's impossible machine: the aeroplane.

Glenn L. Martin built his first successful airplane inside this small church in Santa Ana, Calif., in 1910. [INSET] Assembling the first Martin pusher plane. Note the stained-glass church window in the background.

Malcolm Loughead (left) and Allan Loughead in their F-1 flying boat.

On a Chicago ball field in 1910, 21-year-old Allan Haines Loughead climbed into a spindly collection of wood, fabric, cables, glue, bicycle wheels and a 30hp engine. He had never piloted an aircraft, but he offered 3-to-1 odds to his fellow mechanics that he would be the first to get their Curtiss pusher biplane to fly.

No one took the wager, and anyone betting against Loughead would have lost. He piloted the normally cumbersome craft in a graceful circle and brought it down to a gentle landing. "It was partly nerve, partly confidence and partly damn foolishness," he said years later. "But now I was an aviator."[2] Being a pilot wasn't enough, however. Loughead moved with his brother Malcolm to San Francisco, ready to create a better aircraft.

After the Wright brothers' first powered flight in December 1903, mechanics, tinkerers and inventors around the world tried their hand at the new field of aviation. But three Californians stood out: Allan and Malcolm Loughead and Glenn L. Martin became world-renowned aviation pioneers, leading lives and launching companies that took remarkably parallel paths on the way to becoming a joint force.

After their inaugural flights and initial financial successes, the founders and the companies they led shared many of the same struggles and opportunities through the decades that followed, including early success in commercial and military aviation, exponential growth during World War II, as well as expansion into space and, ultimately, cyberspace. In 1995, these two companies, similar in size and success, formalized their history of parallel experiences with the "merger of equals" that created Lockheed Martin Corporation, a name that honors those original giants of aviation.

OF BIRDS AND BRIDGES

"The aeroplane will take over land and water travel. Flying has no barriers," Allan Loughead said in 1910.[3] Despite these confident words, land and water are some of humanity's oldest barriers. Unfriendly terrain and raging rivers once made land travel a dangerous proposition, and navigating great oceans meant losing months of time and risking hundreds of lives.

From the ancient authors of the Icarus myth to the scientist-artists of the Renaissance, people have dreamed of slipping the bonds of Earth through powered flight. But such flights of fantasy are typically tempered by pragmatism. The promise of flight is the promise of safe and speedy transport, of commercial trade, of military might, of easier

Leonardo da Vinci sketched this helicopter design some 400 years before vertical flight became a reality.

Known as the "birdman," Otto Lilienthal used a mix of scientific scrutiny and showmanship to help inspire many aviators who followed. He died in 1896 in a glider crash.

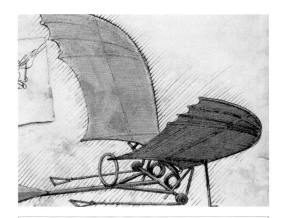

Following both avian and batlike frameworks, da Vinci believed humans might one day fly using contraptions like these.

The Pratt Truss method of bridge construction influenced many of the most popular and successful aeroplane designs of the 1910s.

interpersonal connection. Before the dream of flight was realized, the earliest practical answers to the barriers of land and water were bridges and ships.

Lockheed Martin's legacy includes many national and international organizations — the mergers, acquisitions and partnerships formed during the past 100 years. The earliest of these "heritage companies" is the San Francisco Bridge Company, established in 1886. By the late 1890s, innovations in bridge- and shipbuilding already exerted tremendous influence on the burgeoning field of aviation.

KILL DEVIL HILLS

Wilbur and Orville Wright took the knowledge of scientists, engineers and tinkers around the world and combined it with what they learned to set mankind into flight. The Wrights began experimenting in 1899, using profits from their bicycle shop to fund aeronautical innovations. On December 17, 1903, Orville Wright piloted their Wright Flyer and achieved the world's first powered flight on the sand dunes of Kill Devil Hills in North Carolina. The fourth short flight that day ended in a rough landing that broke the front elevator support. But the dream of manned flight had become a reality.

Dan Tate (left) and Edward Huffaker help launch Wilbur Wright on their 1901 glider in Kitty Hawk.

Over the next five years, the Wrights improved on their invention, but other experimenters kept pace at home and overseas. In 1906, Brazilian-born Alberto Santos-Dumont achieved the first officially recognized flight in Europe with his unique 14-bis. The following year, France's Louis Blériot flew his Blériot VII monoplane 500 meters. By 1908, France's Henri Farman completed Europe's first 1-kilometer circular flight and, later that year, a 17-mile flight across France. Back in the United States, Glenn Hammond Curtiss set records of his own in the Alexander Graham Bell-backed *June Bug*.

With flight a practical, if still extremely risky, proposition, the race was on.

THE DREAM OF MANNED FLIGHT HAD BECOME A REALITY.

Based largely on box-kite construction, Alberto Santos-Dumont's otherworldly 14-bis flew 220 meters in 21 seconds. This illustration is based on a photograph taken during his historic flight on November 12, 1906, in France.

"IS [BLÉRIOT] GOING TO GO UP IN THE AIR IN THIS TINY THING? THE FIRST SEAFARERS HAD HAD IT EASIER. THEY COULD PRACTICE FIRST IN POOLS, THEN IN PONDS, THEN IN STREAMS, AND NOT VENTURE OUT TO SEA UNTIL MUCH LATER. FOR THIS MAN THERE IS ONLY SEA."[4]

— FRANZ KAFKA, "THE AEROPLANES AT BRESCIA," 1909

A WORLD OF AVIATION

Facing intensifying competition from European and American pioneers, the Wright brothers redoubled their efforts to find paying customers for their flying machines. A French business syndicate and the U.S. Army Signal Corps showed early interest and requested public demonstrations. Despite early disasters, military, commercial and popular enthusiasm for flying machines could not be stifled for long.

In July 1909, Louis Blériot bested aviation pioneer Hubert Latham by becoming the first person to cross the English Channel by airplane. The Blériot XI monoplane made the 22-mile journey in high winds before crash-landing near Dover Castle. The daring pilot emerged safely, and his monoplane design, with its front-mounted "tractor" engine, set a new standard for potential military and civilian customers alike.

By 1910, French aircraft manufacturers such as Blériot, Farman and the Voisin brothers were leading the global industry, and German and British producers flourished as well. In the United States, three pioneers were making names for themselves on the golden coast of California.

The similarities between the Lockheed and Martin company founders are uncanny. At a time when aircraft were remarkably difficult to fly, the Loughead brothers and Martin exhibited abundant natural talent as aviators. All were mechanically brilliant and self-taught pioneers in the emerging field of aircraft design. All felt a profound calling to the skies. And all launched their respective companies with the creation of reliable sea planes.

Henri Farman is cheered by onlookers as he wins the Grand Prix d'Aviation on January 13, 1908, completing the first 1-kilometer flight circuit in European history.

French poster commemorating Louis Blériot's historic channel-crossing flight. A Paris newspaper reporter was waiting outside Dover Castle and signaled Blériot with a French flag as he emerged from the fog, one of the earliest air traffic control efforts on record, 1909.

PARALLEL PATHS

Rented for $12 a month, Glenn Martin's church "factory" in Santa Ana, Calif., was as practical as it was symbolically sacred. Stained-glass windows helped him keep his work under wraps. The nave, without its pews, provided a spacious wooden floor with no interior posts. The high ceiling offered ample clearance for the tall airframe. In this workspace, the slim, bespectacled proprietor of Martin Garage lived the second half of his double life. Some nights he worked alone, struggling to hold his lantern while fine-tuning engine parts. Other nights, Martin collaborated with Roy Beall, his chief mechanic, and Charles Day, a mechanics instructor from the local YMCA. Even Glenn's mother, Minta, joined the effort.

After 13 months of work, they were finished. The spruce struts and bamboo tail boom offered a perfect mixture of strength and lightness. The muslin wings were varnished to reinforce and streamline the fabric. Fitted with a 15hp Ford automobile engine and weighing in at 1,150 pounds, Glenn L. Martin's pusher biplane was ready to fly.

Unfortunately, their machine was stuck inside — a ship in a bottle. Martin could dismantle the plane and reassemble it outside, but the process would have taken weeks, and Martin hated the thought of pulling to pieces the machine he'd worked so hard to build. He stood outside, staring at the narrow church doorway. There had to be a better way.

Martin had a stroke of genius. When faced with the logistical puzzle of removing a ship from a bottle, sometimes it's best to break the glass. Rather than dismantle his plane, he persuaded the owner of the Santa Ana church to let him simply slice off the front of the church itself, promising he'd build an enlarged entrance with a new vestibule. The owner agreed. Soon, a midnight procession of townspeople followed Martin's Ford motorcar as it towed the intact biplane to James Irvine's bean field, the site of the aircraft's maiden voyage and Martin's second attempt at flight.

At dawn on August 1, 1910, a lurching, bumpy ride gave way to a moment of peace as Glenn Martin's plane took to the air. After 100 feet of flight, with a top altitude of 8 feet, Martin gently landed his aircraft. The gathered throng swarmed the plane, ecstatically waving their hats and pounding the back of the latest aviation pioneer. Martin still felt like he was floating on air and steadied himself against the trusses of his now-successful aircraft. While Roy Beall and Charles Day went into town to celebrate, Glenn Martin returned home to deliver the good news to his mother and father:

"We got it off the ground," he told them. "It flew."[5]

BUILDING THE MODEL G

Four hundred miles north of Santa Ana, in 1912, Allan Loughead worked in a small garage on the corner of San Francisco's Pacific and Polk streets. He had witnessed and narrowly escaped too many fatal crashes in "pusher" planes, where the engine often ripped off its rear mounting and crushed the pilot, and knew there had to be a better way.

Inspired by the successful Blériot designs, Allan and brother Malcolm designed a wood-and-fabric sea plane — with an 80hp "tractor" motor up front and a single sled-type pontoon below — able to take off and land on bodies of water such as the nearby San Francisco Bay. Only a year earlier, 24-year-old pilot Eugene Ely made history on that very harbor, completing the world's first airplane landing aboard a sea vessel, the USS *Pennsylvania*. Although neither Loughead brother was a trained draftsman, they produced many designs, labeling them A through G, and finally settled on this last option. The Loughead Model G was designed to seat three people — two passengers plus the pilot — and, hopefully, make money. If it worked, this would be the largest sea plane built in America, and they hoped the boating community in San Francisco might pay for the chance to fly above their bay.

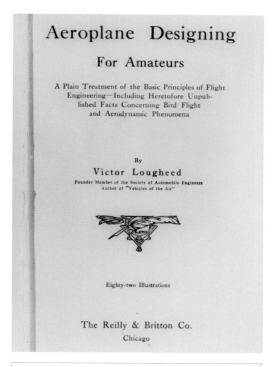

Victor Loughead, older half-brother of Allan and Malcolm, published widely on aviation, including two seminal books. "Vehicles of the Air" was first published in 1909 and reprinted as recently as 1995. "Aeroplane Designing for Amateurs" offered practical advice for a generation of budding aircraft builders, including the younger Lougheads. Victor helped Allan land a job on the Curtiss aircraft fleet in Chicago, but sadly, a rift developed between the brothers that was never reconciled.

The Loughead Model G on its launching ramp. The pontoon advertises the Alco Hydro-Aeroplane Company, offering exposure for their primary investor and owner of the local Alco Cab Company, Max Mamlock, 1912.

Although the tractor plane might be marginally safer for its passengers, there were still many risks and challenges involved for the Loughead brothers, including the constant problem of capital. Allan and Malcolm secured a $1,200 investment from the local Alco Cab Company, supplementing the $2,800 that came from their own pockets and those of smaller investors. On December 19, 1912, with financing in place, the brothers incorporated the Alco-Hydro Aeroplane Company.

In the small garage where they repaired cars during the day, the brothers' aircraft took shape. They had to build the plane strong enough to withstand the temperamental San Francisco weather. If the plane did crash into the bay, the pieces could not be salvaged and their investment would be lost. To cap it off, Allan's wife was pregnant, and they were depending on the Model G for their livelihood.

MARTIN MODEL 12

On May 10, 1912, Glenn L. Martin stood on a dock in Newport Bay, Calif., and solemnly handed his gold pocket watch to engineer Charlie Day. "Take care of this," the 26-year-old barnstorming aviator said, "in case I go for a swim."[6]

Martin was attempting to break the distance record for flight across open water, setting his sights on Catalina Island. Thirty-four miles of ocean lay between him and his destination, a considerably greater distance than Blériot's 22-mile flight over the English Channel. Glenn's mother, Minta, slipped an inflated bicycle inner tube over his neck, just in case. He guided his team as they mounted a pontoon beneath a Martin Model 12 aircraft. After a quick wave to his parents and colleagues on the dock, he took off, climbing to an estimated 4,000 feet. As he approached 30 minutes in flight, his compass work impeccable, he broke through some ominous cloud cover to find Catalina's Avalon Bay directly in front of him. He touched down safely, but a group of young men dragged his plane onto Catalina's gravely shores, tearing a hole in his pontoon. It took five hours for a local yachtsman to patch it. Upon takeoff for the return flight, the patch tore open. Bringing all of his barnstorming skills to bear, he splashed down nose high as close to the shore as possible. With the pontoon quickly taking on water, the plane came to a stop just as the waterline reached the bottom of its wing.

He set two world records: the longest hydroplane flight and the longest round-trip flight over water. But Martin had other concerns.

Glenn L. Martin in the pusher sea plane with which he made his record 34-mile, 37-minute flight from Newport Bay to Catalina Island on May 10, 1912, breaking Louis Blériot's channel-crossing record. In this photo, he carries a passenger, 1912.

"Charlie, what have you done with my watch?" he yelled.

Day had dashed shoulder-deep into the surf to help beach the plane; the watch in his pocket was ruined. But with two world records, it seemed more than an even trade.

International acclaim soon followed, and so too did the formal incorporation of the Glenn L. Martin Company, on August 16, 1912. Martin moved out of the church and into a small factory at 943 S. Los Angeles St. in downtown L.A.

INTERNATIONAL ACCLAIM SOON FOLLOWED.

Martin's Los Angeles pontoon operation, 1912.

The wood-and-fabric Model G sea plane is launched, 1913.

The Loughead Model G flew over San Francisco Bay during the international Panama-Pacific Exposition of 1915, affording its passengers an aerial view not unlike the one illustrated in this poster.

A PROFITABLE PLANE

On the first day of June 1913, Allan Loughead's wife Dorothy gave birth to their first child, a daughter named Flora. Allan's family was now riding on the fate of an untested sea plane. It simply had to fly.

Two weeks after Flora's birth, on June 15, Allan and Malcolm launched their Model G from a boat ramp near Fort Mason into the San Francisco Bay. Allan pushed the throttle. Soon, the plane was airborne. Lockheed's first flight of the Model G was in the books.

Malcolm joined Allan for the second flight, soaring to an altitude of 300 feet over Alcatraz Island and Sausalito Bay, to the delight of onlookers.

But the challenges didn't abate. When the plane was damaged months later, their anxious Alco investor seized it and placed it in storage. To earn enough money to repair it and buy it back, the Loughead brothers turned to their old day jobs as mechanics and tried panning for gold in California. Malcolm even served as an adviser for the single-plane air force of a revolutionary general in Mexico (where a Martin-built aircraft also saw service). It took more than a year, but the brothers recovered and repaired the craft just in time for the 1915 Panama-Pacific Exposition.

The international gathering was a huge success. The Lougheads sold flights to more than 600 people for the dizzying sum of $10 a ride, all without incident or injury. The Model G had now accomplished something truly innovative: It had turned a profit.

In 1916, the brothers moved near their mother in Santa Barbara, Calif., and established the Loughead Aircraft Manufacturing Company in a garage at 101 State St., mere blocks away from the waterfront.

PREPARING FOR WAR

Tensions in France, Great Britain and Germany ran high in summer 1911 as the three powers squared off when France deployed troops to quell a rebellion in Morocco, breaking the Franco-German Accord of 1909. The presence of German gunboats alarmed the British, who feared the possibility of a German naval base on the Atlantic Ocean. The standoff ended, but a major war seemed imminent.

The United States was not yet preparing for what would become World War I, but the military's lack of planes or trained pilots was nonetheless becoming a glaring deficiency. In 1913, the Army Signal Corps sent aeronautical engineer Grover C. Loening to the few domestic aircraft manufacturers, including Glenn Martin's Los Angeles plant. At the time, Martin was making money primarily through flying exhibitions and running an aviation school (his students included William Edward Boeing). Loening was looking for a machine that could hold two people — flight instructor and student — with controls for both and a tractor propeller rather than the more dangerous pusher variety. Loening rattled off additional speed and altitude specifications, and then asked for a finished product in six weeks.

Martin and his chief engineer Charles Willard were already working on an aircraft surprisingly similar to the one Loening described. Within six weeks' time, they delivered to the Army the Martin TT (Tractor Trainer), the first plane designed for military training. The TT also marked the first military contract won by the fledgling Martin Company, setting a precedent of military aviation support that would extend through the coming century.

The Martin T accommodated instructor and student side by side. Planes like the Martin T became useful for aerial photography and even served as leading players in the burgeoning California film industry. Here, Glenn Martin (back) strokes actress Mary Pickford's hair in the 1915 film *The Girl of Yesterday*.

The Model S Hydroplane was a single-float sea plane version of the TT. With two destroyers in the background, Navy personnel help guide the S into the water. Note the expanded gap between the fuselage and the lower wing.

The Army marveled at the TT and ordered 14 more in 1914. These planes were used to train 29 pilots and delivered an extraordinary improvement on the Army's previous safety record. Martin later flew the TT on the Army's first official bombardment experiments in San Diego.

A VISION OF THE FUTURE

Three days after Germany invaded Belgium, Glenn Martin offered a prophetic vision of military aviation in the August 7, 1914, issue of the Los Angeles Evening Herald. "The aeroplane will practically decide the war in Europe," he said. "For the old-time war tactics are no more. The generals who realize this quickest … will win."[7]

While the lasting and ubiquitous images of "dogfights" may be more propaganda than reality, German, French, Dutch and British aerial aces such as Manfred von Richthofen ("The Red Baron") and Raoul Lufbery symbolized a more glorified counterpoint to the inhuman horrors of chemical and trench warfare.

Martin described the three distinct types of airplanes he predicted the military would use: low-speed, high-payload bombers; slightly faster reconnaissance aircraft; and high-speed fighter planes. Aircraft were, in fact, used for observation and reconnaissance in World War I, and aircraft with machine guns or explosives dropped by hand were the earliest bombers and fighter planes.

Though Martin's military foresight was impressively accurate, he neglected to mention a fourth type of military airplane: the transport aircraft.

LOUGHEAD F-1 FLYING BOAT

In early 1916, the newly formed Loughead Aircraft Manufacturing Company began work on its follow-up to the profitable Model G sea plane, figuring that "if the three-seat Model G could make money, a ten-seat aircraft would be even more profitable."[8]

As a small group of employees labored over the design in their Santa Barbara garage, they noticed a young man lingering at the entrance. The 20-year-old would-be engineer was John K. Northrop. Working on the new flying-boat design with the Lougheads, Northrop "drew up the wing truss structure, designed and stress analyzed it and did every bit of the drawing … necessary for the airplane."[9] The distinctive design of the F-1 flying boat, constructed under the direction of Anthony Stadlman, Allan Loughead's colleague from his barnstorming days in Chicago, boasted a 74-foot upper wingspan, two 150hp engines, twin booms and a triple tail. The bold undertaking paid off commercially, but Malcolm and Allan Loughead both foresaw the potential military value of their aircraft as well, offering their plant and services to the U.S. government "in event of trouble with any foreign power."[10]

Indeed, when America entered the war on April 6, 1917, and Northrop became a private in the Army Signal Corps, Allan traveled to Washington, D.C., to secure a larger military contract for the F-1. He returned only with a contract to produce two Curtiss HS-2L flying boats, as well as an offer for the Navy to test the F-1. Still, with these opportunities in his pocket, Loughead hired Stadlman as factory superintendent and secured Northrop's release from the Signal Corps, offering him a salaried engineer position in Santa Barbara. Northrop rejoined a growing workforce of 85 men working a wartime production schedule, seven days a week.

Cockpit of the twin-engine F-1 flying boat, which sat 10 passengers, 1918.

Malcolm Loughead stands in a gun turret while Norman S. Hall, Anthony Stadlman, Berton R. Rodman, Allan Loughead and John K. Northrop (left to right) pose in front of the Loughead-built Curtiss HS-2L flying boat.

Over a year later, on April 12, it completed a record-setting nonstop flight to San Diego for its naval testing, flying 211 miles in only 181 minutes. Regrettably, the Navy had already ordered a sufficient number of Curtiss planes and decided not to buy the F-1. The Lougheads had arrived too late, learning a tough but valuable lesson: When it comes to supporting the military, timing counts just as much as innovation.

MERGER MISFIRE

Glenn L. Martin, too, learned this lesson the hard way during World War I.

Despite the success of the Martin TT and its variations, larger auto manufacturers won most of the war production contracts, primarily for non-U.S.-designed airplanes. Meanwhile, the war-weary British and Dutch were looking across the pond for possible sources of aircraft production. When Dutch aviator Lt. H. Ter Poorten visited Martin's Los Angeles operation, he promptly persuaded his government to order 20 airplanes. It was the Martin Company's first foreign contract.

Glenn Martin had recently hired 23-year-old Donald Douglas to replace Charles Willard as chief engineer. Douglas helped modify the Model TT into the Model R sea plane. Three of these were delivered to the Navy in 1917, marking Martin's first naval contract.

Still, work was scarce. In late summer 1916, Martin jumped on what seemed a surefire opportunity to merge with the Wright Company to form the Wright-Martin Company, formally renamed on November 19, 1916. Only the large Curtiss operation could now compete with the consolidated Wright-Martin enterprise, or so they thought.

The merger didn't last. The wartime Aircraft Production Board exerted political and operational control over Martin's efforts, repurposing the Los Angeles plant for the production of third-party engines, and replacing Douglas with Chance Milton Vought without Martin's approval or consultation. Martin saw himself pigeonholed into the role of figurehead. He needed a way out.

He found his escape hatch in Cleveland. Alva Bradley, owner of the Cleveland Indians baseball team, arranged the financing for Martin to re-form his company and move his plant to Ohio. Less than a year after its formation, the Wright-Martin Corporation

> WHEN IT COMES TO SUPPORTING THE MILITARY, TIMING COUNTS JUST AS MUCH AS INNOVATION.

FIRST LADIES OF FLIGHT

THOUGH THE AGE OF THE FAMOUS FEMALE AVIATOR HAD NOT YET DAWNED, SEVERAL BRAVE AND BOLD WOMEN SUPPORTED AND INFLUENCED THE LOUGHEAD AND MARTIN COMPANIES THROUGHOUT THE 1910s.

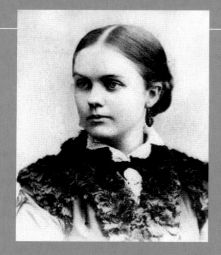

Always encouraging, Minta Martin was perhaps the world's first mother to be flown in the air by her son. As a boy, Glenn used to cut his mother's bedsheets to build sails and kites, and Minta supported his experiments for decades to come. "It was my mother who encouraged me to believe in myself," Glenn Martin said in 1943.[11]

In addition to designing and building aircraft, Martin patented what was then called a "safety pack" with a parachute deployment system that pilots could comfortably wear and safely engage when needed. Here, Georgia "Tiny" Broadwick hangs astride a Model T piloted by Glenn L. Martin as she prepares to test a Martin parachute design in 1913. According to the San Francisco newspaper The Call, the demonstration was a success. "For the first time in the history of aviation a woman has made a descent from a rapidly moving aeroplane to the earth in perfect safety," it reported.[12]

The so-called "Mother of Lockheed," Flora Haines Loughead, was a remarkably resourceful and prolific author, miner and farmer. Having married, divorced and moved the family several times — as well as prospecting her own claims into her 80s — Flora's pioneering spirit surely rubbed off on her sons.

was finished. Martin rehired Douglas, and a newly incorporated Glenn L. Martin Company was formed on September 19, 1917, in Cleveland. Immediately, they got to work on their first aircraft design: a fast twin-engine bomber.

MARTIN BOMBERS

Time was of the essence. Glenn Martin knew he had built the most advanced bomber the world had ever seen, the MB-1. He was itching to show it off to the U.S. government. So in September 1918, two weeks before military officials expected him, he climbed aboard his new bomber and settled in as his pilot, Eric Springer, took off for McCook Field in Dayton, Ohio.

But when the massive aircraft safely landed at McCook, everyone on the plane was immediately arrested. The war in Europe had set the guards on edge. The bomber's arrival was unscheduled, and no one on the ground had ever seen an aircraft quite like it: a hulking 10,000-pound wood-framed biplane with a dramatic 72-foot wingspan. Amid the chaos, Martin convinced the guards that this was the plane their commanders had ordered.

Captain Rudolph "Shorty" Schroeder, an ace military pilot, was dispatched to take the MB-1 up for a test flight. An hour later, after challenging it to every aerial test he could think of, Schroeder returned with nothing but praise. The MB-1 became the first American-made bomber purchased by the U.S. Army.

But the war was waning. The Army's initial order of 50 MB-1s dropped to just 16 by war's end in November, and Martin fielded smaller orders from the U.S. Postal Service and the Navy. Engineers began work on a redesign of the MB-1, which traded off speed and handling for the ability to carry a heavier payload.

Impressed, the Army placed an order for 20 of Martin's more powerful bombers, the MB-2, in January 1919. But critics remained skeptical of the efficacy of aerial bombing and questioned whether an aircraft could drop a bomb large enough to damage naval vessels.

To prove the concept in 1921, air power's greatest champion, Brig. Gen. William "Billy" Mitchell, made Martin's MB-2 his aircraft of choice. Anchored off the

The first Martin MB-1 is assembled in the company's new Cleveland facility.

… NO ONE ON THE GROUND HAD EVER SEEN AN AIRCRAFT QUITE LIKE IT. …

"A BOMB THAT WAS FIRED TODAY WILL BE HEARD AROUND THE WORLD."

—MAJ. GEN. CLARENCE C. WILLIAMS, 1921

From left, Lawrence Bell, Eric Springer, Glenn L. Martin and Donald Douglas stand in front of a completed MB-1, 1918.

Virginia coast, four captured German ships from World War I were positioned for an aerial bombardment. Among them was the massive *Ostfriedland*, considered unsinkable. Early runs easily sank the smaller ships in minutes, including a German submarine, but Mitchell offered one more display of the MB-2's unprecedented ability. Seven MB-2s outfitted to carry newly developed 1-ton bombs showered the *Ostfriedland* with their payloads, dispatching it to the bottom of the Atlantic Ocean in just over 20 minutes. In response, Maj. Gen. Clarence C. Williams, the Army's chief of ordnance, declared, "A bomb that was fired today will be heard around the world."[13]

Martin's excitement over Mitchell's bomb tests would be short-lived. Under the contract system of the day, the Army Air Service had the right to purchase the designs to the MB-2 and dole out production to the bidders who came in below Martin's asking price.

Thus, the initial order of 20 MB-2 bombers would be the only one Martin would fill for the Army. Over the next 10 years, however, the company would produce more than 400 aircraft for the U.S. Navy alone, including its first all-metal sea plane, the MO-1, as well as the successful T3M and T4M torpedo bombers, which proved the Glenn L. Martin Company was adept at creating bombers for use over both land and sea.

A Martin MB-2 drops a 1-ton bomb on the captured German battleship *Ostfriedland*, 1921.

Advertisement for the short-lived S-1 Sport biplane.

PEACETIME PRODUCTION

In the postwar economy, recession set in, hitting the aviation production industry especially hard. With $600 in his pocket, Donald Douglas left the Martin Company in 1920 to return to California, where flying was possible year-round. Meanwhile, Glenn Martin championed the value of peacetime production of military technology, stating in 1920:

> It is immediately evident that the industrial strength of the United States must be at the war strength all the time, as production of aircraft cannot be developed under one year from any given date. Therefore the government must stimulate and aid in the application of aircraft industrially, and also aid in foreign trade, furnishing sufficient outlet for industrial aviation and guaranteeing a continuity of production at the required rate.[14]

While Martin focused on military customers, the Lougheads once again turned to the potential of civilian and sporting markets. On July 18, 1919, Allan and Malcolm Loughead, John Northrop and Anthony Stadlman signed a formal agreement to share in all patents and inventions, and to determine together which new patents should be

The S-1 Sport biplane employed several innovative features, including a patented monocoque fuselage with no internal bracing. It also featured folding wings for easier ground transportation.

THE TRUSTY

One of the few military aircraft successes of the 1920s came from the Lockheed Martin heritage company Consolidated Aircraft Corporation of Buffalo, N.Y. After the Martin TT, the Army was looking for a new primary training aircraft and selected the Consolidated PT-1. With a metal fuselage framework of chrome-molybdenum steel tubing, the PT-1 was a stark departure from the all-wood construction of earlier trainers. Easily maneuverable and structurally sturdy, the PT-1 soon earned the nickname *Trusty*.

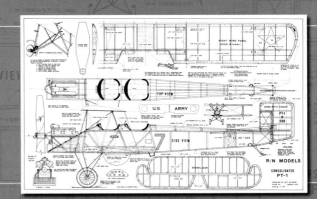

developed. The foursome soon decided that the future of aviation was an "'every-man's airplane'. … a safe, simple, inexpensive aircraft that would be the aeronautical equivalent of the Ford Model T."[15]

In 1919, the Loughead Aircraft Manufacturing Company designed and built the revolutionary S-1 Sportplane. Seeking a sturdier fuselage that could fly faster and handle the stresses of flight more predictably, the company patented an innovative production process for a molded plywood fuselage. Meanwhile, Northrop's observation of natural phenomena brought about another breakthrough in aviation that led to safer landings at lower speeds. He spread breadcrumbs near the waterfront and observed how gulls used the lower parts of their wings as an air brake. The S-1 design was the first to incorporate this insight into avian flight, with flaps that could change the aerodynamic profile of the wing while in flight. Nearly every aircraft today has followed suit.

Despite its design breakthroughs, the S-1 did not sell. The glut of cheap war surplus Curtiss JN-4s meant that planes were often available for as little as $300. Despite the fact that the S-1 handled very well and was cheap to operate and maintain, the $2,500 tag priced the S-1 out of the "everyman" market.

The danger inherent in postwar barnstorming events both inspired and frightened Americans, but nonetheless spread the gospel of "air-mindedness" far and wide.

BARNSTORMING AND TRAILBLAZING

In the early 1920s, many so-called "everymen" were unemployed. Some of the jobless military aviators found work as Hollywood stunt pilots, crop dusters, air mail carriers and aerial surveyors. Others performed daring public stunts — known as "barnstorming" — in cheap war surplus planes that were often in ill repair, making barnstorming a dangerous endeavor. Because of the expendability of these planes, many were crashed on purpose to liven up a show. Parachuting, wing-walking and other daredevil stunts introduced hundreds of local communities to the excitement of aviation. The notion of public "air-mindedness" became a postwar rally cry.

In Europe, a more mature commercial aviation industry focused on blazing new trails in the "highway in the sky." Pioneering flights tested travel routes, weather systems, landing sites and trade opportunities. In America, these efforts were led by a formalized air mail service established in 1919 from New York to Cleveland, and then on to Chicago, before expanding farther west in 1920. The French Aéropostale service also began air mail flights in 1919 but covered considerably greater ground, extending by 1927 to South America. These air mail efforts paved the way for an era of commercial aviation.

Meanwhile, a massive global threat was germinating in postwar Europe. In 1922, Benito Mussolini established his dictatorship in Italy. Three years later, the publication of Adolf Hitler's *Mein Kampf* marked another early foothold of fascism in Europe and planted the seeds for World War II. In America, the Roaring '20s saw a resurgence in enthusiasm for aviation. Corporations and governments again offered prizes and held events that publicized feats of speed, altitude and distance. Crossing the Atlantic Ocean remained the golden goose. With the turmoil of World War I in the past, America focused on a new crop of daring pilot-explorers who would usher in the Golden Age of aviation.

After World War I, unemployed pilots traveled the country, treating small-town America to wing-walking, aerial trickery and other feats of daring.

CHAPTER 2

SMALL FACTORIES

The Golden Age of Aviation

1926-1937

"THERE HAS NEVER BEEN A SENSATION MORE
SOUL-SATISFYING THAN THE FIRST FLIGHT OF A NEW
DESIGN; NO FIELD OF ENDEAVOR HALF SO FASCINATING
AS THE CHALLENGE OF EACH NEW SECRET OF FLIGHT."[1]

—GLENN L. MARTIN

WOOD AND METAL

In Hollywood, Calif., spiral strips of spruce were laminated and coated with glue, then bonded overnight under 150 tons of pressure. Once these hulls were completed, they would be clean, sleek, amazingly customizable and stronger than steel. It was 1926, and the Lockheed Vega was taking shape. It would soon redefine civilian aviation.

The Lockheed Aircraft Company's monocoque hulls for a Model 1 Vega under assembly. On the far side of the fuselage is Chief Engineer Gerard Vultee (wearing suspenders) and Treasurer W. Kenneth Jay, c. 1928. [INSET] In 1918, the Glenn L. Martin Company's 61,000-square-foot plant in Cleveland was built in only 45 days under the direction of factory manager Lawrence Bell, who also designed the company's star emblem, 1918.

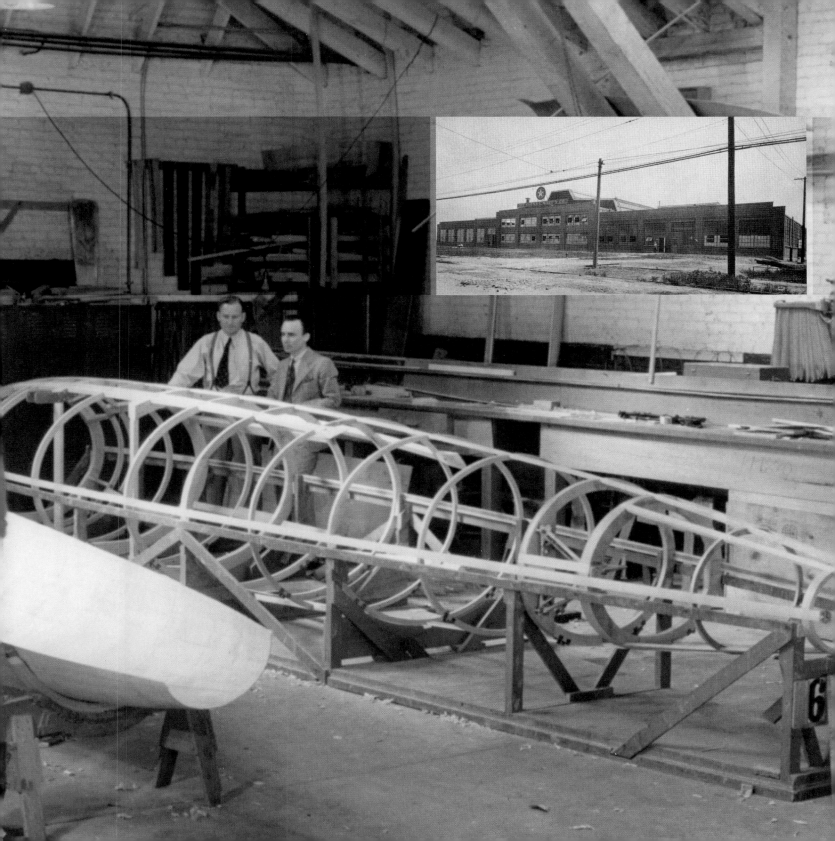

The Glenn L. Martin Company's T3M-1 (Model 73) torpedo-bomber-scout plane was the third in a series of three-purpose naval planes, following the SC-1 and SC-2. In the Cleveland plant, the aircraft's uncovered metal fuselage frame is seen with engineers in crew positions, 1926.

More than 2,000 miles away, in Cleveland, welded steel tubing framed positions for pilot, bomber, gunner and radio operator. After the fuselage was finished, it was fitted with one of the industry's new air-cooled radial engines, providing improved power. The Glenn L. Martin Company would ultimately build more than 300 "three-purpose" (torpedo-bomber-scout) planes like the T4M-1 and its variants, supplying aircraft to the U.S. Navy's carriers for the better part of a decade.

The period known as aviation's Golden Age broke the boundaries of commercial, private and military aviation. Pioneering pilots were among the biggest household names of the Roaring '20s, and their record-setting feats ushered in a period of public "air-mindedness." Sparked by impresarios, businesses and governments around the world, the aircraft created during this period served many purposes for many customers. In this rarified atmosphere, the Lockheed and Martin companies weathered financial storms and staked their claim as industry leaders.

A NEW NAME, A NEW COMPANY

The failure of the S-1 Sportplane in the early 1920s presaged the end of the Loughead Aircraft Manufacturing Company, but its four leaders separated on amicable terms.

Malcolm Loughead, who had patented a four-wheel hydraulic brake system, moved to Detroit to focus on the booming automobile industry. Tired of people mispronouncing his name as "Log-head," Malcolm officially changed his surname to "Lockheed" and founded the Lockheed Hydraulic Brake Company. Allan also changed his name and became Malcolm's California distributor, still working in his spare time on new ideas for aircraft. Engineer Jack Northrop moved to Santa Monica to work for Glenn L. Martin's former chief engineer, Donald Douglas, at the Douglas Aircraft Company.

Lighter air-cooled engines foreshadowed the future of powered flight, and daring aviators continued testing the newest innovations during public spectacles. Investors looked for opportunities to get in on the ground floor of the aircraft business, which they hoped would follow the fast-growing automobile business as the next growth market.

In the mid-1920s, Jack Northrop designed innovative cantilevered monoplanes for California manufacturers such as Ryan, as well as Allan Lockheed. The cantilever, a

Built in the early 1920s, an uncovered Martin MO-1 showcases an all-metal framework. The wing shows certain structural similarities to the Vega's cantilevered approach, but the aluminum alloy materials were a striking departure from the Vega's all-wood construction.

Employees pose next to a cantilevered Vega wing during construction, 1930.

"I LIVE ONLY IN THE MOMENT IN THIS STRANGE UNMORTAL SPACE, CROWDED WITH BEAUTY, PIERCED WITH DANGER."[2]

—CHARLES LINDBERGH

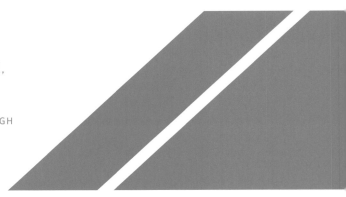

Allan Lockheed, John K. Northrop, Anthony Stadlman and Gerard Vultee laying out plans for the new Lockheed Vega, 1927.

wooden strut inside a thicker upper wing, marked a significant step from biplane to monoplane. Lockheed was initially against the cantilevered approach, but Northrop held his ground, sure that "a stoutly built plywood-covered wooden cantilever wing without the usual multiplicity of struts was essential to the clean lines he sought."[3] In addition, they crafted an incredibly light but durable fuselage by lining concrete molds with laminated spiral strips of vertical-grain spruce, in the revolutionary monocoque production process from the S-1.

The SC-2 dropping its torpedo from a height of 12 feet. Martin built 40 of these torpedo-bomber-scout planes, underbidding Curtiss for the production contract, 1926.

Thirteen T3M-2s on the flight line at NAS North Island, Calif., in 1928.

The T4M-1 radio operator had a rear-firing ventral machine gun, shown here in the fuselage framework, 1928.

Glenn Martin (left) and Charles Lindbergh, 1928.

The resulting cigar-shaped fuselage, as solid as the ribs of a cargo boat, could carry a heavy, more powerful engine — up to 650 hp — that could allow the aircraft to reach much higher speeds. The design for the new Vega, named after one of the brightest stars in the sky, helped secure financing for a reorganized Lockheed venture.

With advice from accountant W. Kenneth Jay and startup capital from brick and tile manufacturer Fred S. Keeler, the new Lockheed Aircraft Company formed in December 1926. Work started on the Vega in a former pottery factory in Hollywood.

"LUCKY" TIMING

While the start of 1927 was an exciting if turbulent time for the new Lockheed company, the Martin company enjoyed relative stability. After winning a contract to produce 35 SC-1 torpedo planes, Martin so pleased the Navy with both the price and production of the aircraft that the government ordered 40 of an improved version, the SC-2. The Navy bought another 230 of this multipurpose model and its subsequent versions between 1927 and 1930, making Martin one of the largest aircraft manufacturers in the United States.

Meanwhile, a much smaller operation was about to make headlines. In February 1927, Claude Ryan received an order for a modified single-engine monoplane with massive fuel tanks — an aircraft capable of flying nonstop across the Atlantic Ocean. Attempts to fly overseas had already claimed the lives of six pilots. Now, a 25-year-old air mail pilot named Charles A. Lindbergh — dubbed "Lucky Lindy" for having parachuted to safety multiple times after hitting bad weather or running out of fuel — was attempting the impossible, spurred on by the promise of the $25,000 Orteig Prize.

In his custom Ryan NYP *Spirit of St. Louis*, Lindbergh carried 450 gallons of fuel for his journey from New York to Paris. Glenn Martin was in Newark when he heard news of Lindbergh's flight, and along with most of the world, he stayed glued to the airwaves, tracking the young pilot's progress. After more than 3,600 miles and 33 sleepless hours, Lindbergh landed in Paris on May 21, 1927. In all the excitement, Martin missed his train back to Cleveland. He knew that the world was forever changed, and America's new hero had brought his country along with him to the forefront of global aviation.

After Charles Lindbergh's historic flight, sales increased dramatically for both the Lockheed and Martin companies. The timing was finally right for both Martin and Lockheed to introduce their new aircraft models to the world.

THE VEGA RIDES THE LINDBERGH WAVE

On Independence Day 1927, a striking new airplane — sleeker but sturdier than any of its contemporaries — taxied onto a runway, carrying test pilot Eddie Bellande and the uncertain fate of the Lockheed Aircraft Company squarely on its graceful cantilevered wings.

Following Charles Lindbergh's landmark flight just two months earlier, the plane arrived amid unprecedented aeronautical fever. For the right company with the right airplane design, there was not only money to be made but also a special place in the history books.

After a smooth takeoff and an hour in the air, Bellande landed safely and announced, "Boys, she's a dandy. A real joy to fly."[4] Bellande was the first of many pilots to fall in love with the sleek new plane. The Lockheed Vega and the models it inspired compiled impressive speed, distance and altitude records, set by a collection of the world's most recognized ambassadors of air-mindedness.

Eddie Bellande was the test pilot who flew the first Vega from Mines Field, a large hayfield in Inglewood, Calif., 1927.

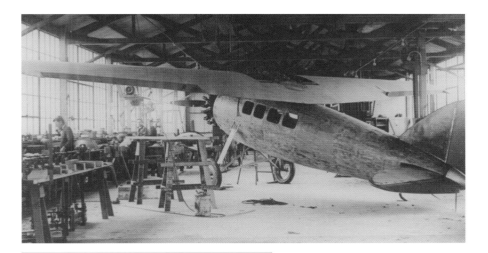

The Vega under construction in Hollywood, Calif., 1927.

FOR THE RIGHT COMPANY WITH THE RIGHT AIRPLANE DESIGN, THERE WAS NOT ONLY MONEY TO BE MADE BUT ALSO A SPECIAL PLACE IN THE HISTORY BOOKS.

FROM DOWN UNDER TO THE TOP OF THE WORLD

Australian-born explorer George Hubert Wilkins was determined to fly over the North Pole, despite having lost five airplanes in the quest. Gazing serendipitously out of a San Francisco hotel room window in August 1927, Wilkins caught a glimpse of a Vega test flight. He immediately rushed out and purchased one, envisioning his Vega as a groundbreaking scientific instrument for exploration of Arctic air routes.

A few months later, he flew the orange and blue Vega *Detroit News*, equipped with landing skis instead of wheels, to Barrow, on Alaska's north coast. In April 1928, flying his Vega through blinding blizzards and temperatures as low as minus 48 degrees Fahrenheit, Wilkins and his co-pilot, Ben Eielson, made an emergency landing on an island off Norway, just short of their destination. Trapped in the Vega for four

days, they waited out the blizzard on emergency rations. When the snow finally stopped, they dug out their airplane and created a makeshift runway. The long-idled Vega was down to its last 10 gallons of fuel, but they got it airborne and made the five-mile flight to safety.

The miraculous adventure made headlines in The New York Times, garnered Wilkins and Eielson the Harmon Trophy for the most outstanding aeronautical achievement of 1928, and thrust the Lockheed Vega into the public eye. The newly knighted Sir George Hubert Wilkins succeeded in mapping out early Arctic air routes and subsequently surveyed some 100,000 miles of previously uncharted territory in the Antarctic, christening one mountain range "Lockheed" in honor of the company that built his airplane of choice.

The third Vega produced, which was flown by Sir George Hubert Wilkins and Ben Eielson on Arctic and Antarctic expeditions, 1928.

MAKING MOVES

After the publicity of George Hubert Wilkins' Arctic flight, Vega orders poured in. Fred S. Keeler, one of Lockheed's backers, helped the company secure 20,000 square feet of factory space in Burbank, Calif., and the company relocated. Ready to focus on the growing trend of metal aircraft, Jack Northrop left Lockheed to form his own company. Gerard Vultee replaced him as chief engineer in June 1928. Lockheed Aircraft Company went public a month later.

Production of the star aircraft ramped up quickly. The two Vegas produced in 1927 jumped to 29 the following year, with a high-water mark of 60 planes produced in 1929. The aircraft industry took off on Wall Street as much as on the nation's runways. Stocks went through the roof, and aircraft sales soared from $21 million in 1927 to $71 million in 1929.

As predicted, aviation became the hot growth industry, setting off a series of mergers and acquisitions among the biggest aircraft manufacturers. In July 1929, the Detroit Aircraft Corporation bought 87 percent of Lockheed's assets and reorganized Lockheed as a division of the consolidated venture. Allan Lockheed wanted nothing to do with this takeover, but Keeler, Lockheed's majority stockholder, accepted the deal, perhaps foreseeing the coming financial storm. Allan promptly sold his stock and resigned to form the Loughead Brothers Aircraft Corporation (reverting to the original spelling for legal reasons).

In the coming years, Lockheed became one of a small handful of companies to successfully focus on commercial aircraft, while the Glenn L. Martin Company concentrated on military customers, who provided more than $2 million in sales each year.

Martin's success with Navy contracts pointed toward a bright future in the production of sea planes and carrier-based aircraft, but the Cleveland factory lacked year-round access to open water. Although community leaders implored Martin to stay, the company was growing quickly and needed to be closer to the ocean. It was time to make a move. The company settled on Middle River, Md., which offered proximity to a thriving Baltimore, the harbors of the Chesapeake Bay, the expansive Atlantic Ocean and, most importantly, military customers in the nation's capital.

Sir George Hubert Wilkins was knighted after his Arctic flight and explored the Antarctic in his Vega later that same year, naming a mountain range in Lockheed's honor, 1928.

The first PM-1 (Model 117) is launched from the Martin ramp at Dark Head Cove in Middle River, Md. The U.S. Navy ordered 27 of the patrol bombers, and three were delivered to Brazil as PM-1Bs, 1930.

Jack Northrop (standing left of engine) checks over the Vega before the aircraft's initial flight from Mines Field, now part of Los Angeles International Airport, July 4, 1927.

Assembly line with Vega monocoque fuselages in the early production days in Burbank, Calif., 1930.

The massive plant opened in fall 1929. Only three weeks later, the country was reeling from the stock market crash of Black Tuesday. As the Great Depression set in, Martin hoped to maintain his military contracts by producing a new line of dive bombers.

Meanwhile, aeronautical luminaries including Amelia Earhart, Charles Lindbergh and Wiley Post used the Vega to shatter speed and distance records, and establish the first passenger plane routes to South America and Asia. The aircraft's many speed records prompted Allan Lockheed to coin the phrase, "It takes a Lockheed to beat a Lockheed," a statement fitting not only for the iconic Vega but for generations of revolutionary Lockheed planes that would follow.[5]

FLYING BLIND WITH JIMMY DOOLITTLE

The airplane ascended from the foggy runway at Mitchel Field on Long Island no differently than any other airplane would have in September 1929. One glance into the cockpit, however, proved this flight was anything but ordinary. In the front seat, Ben Kelsey stretched his arms into the air to prove he was not controlling the airplane, and a canvas hood covered the rear cockpit, preventing pilot James H. Doolittle from seeing the outside world.

Doolittle, one of the best-known pilots of the era, was attempting the world's first "blind" airplane flight, relying on experimental devices from the Sperry Company to safely guide him home. Sperry engineers had created the world's first airplane guidance system, a revolutionary instrument panel allowing pilots to fly for the first time with poor visibility or in bad weather.

The panel contained two key elements. The first device, called an "attitude" indicator, provided an artificial horizon for guidance when the actual horizon could not be seen. The second instrument, a directional gyroscope, allowed pilots to direct their planes along a precise route. Combined, the two

"IN THE DEPRESSION, PEOPLE WANTED IDOLS TO DISTRACT THEM FROM EVERYDAY REALITY. AVIATION WAS AN ALTERNATIVE. AVIATION WAS LITERALLY HEAVENLY COMPARED TO WHAT WAS GOING ON HERE ON EARTH."[6]

—GORE VIDAL, SON OF EUGENE VIDAL, DIRECTOR OF THE BUREAU OF AIR COMMERCE

eliminated the need for landmarks, transforming flight from a risky daytime pursuit into a reliable form of transportation that could run according to strict schedules.

Doolittle flew "blind" through the fog for 15 minutes in a loose 15-mile oval before setting his NY-2 biplane trainer down in a large grassy field while still under the canvas. The instrument panel designed by Sperry in an aircraft built by Consolidated, both Lockheed Martin legacy companies, ushered in a new age of long-distance flight.

Jimmy Doolittle and his Lockheed Orion Model 9 Shellightning, 1934.

Amelia Earhart captured the world speed record and was the first woman to complete a solo transatlantic flight.

Famous aviator Amelia Earhart, Lockheed Vice President and Sales Manager Carl Squier, and Lockheed President and General Manager Lloyd Stearman at the Lockheed hangar in Burbank, Calif., 1930.

Amelia Earhart was perhaps the world's most famous female aviator. She established many of her world records in a Lockheed Aircraft, 1935.

AMELIA THE AVIATOR

In 1930, a modernized version of the Vega 5C, the DL-1, captured the interest of world-famous aviator Amelia Earhart. Earhart had served as a crew member on a transatlantic flight completed by the Fokker Friendship in 1928. She immediately became a star, thanks in part to the publicity efforts of her publisher, manager and future husband, George P. Putnam. Despite her fame, Earhart felt like little more than a "sack of potatoes" on the transatlantic trip and dreamed of completing the journey as a pilot rather than a passenger.[7]

In June 1930, Earhart borrowed the DL-1 and set three new women's speed records with it. One of Amelia Earhart's primary competitors for record-setting feats was Ruth Nichols, who piloted a Vega to multiple women's world speed, altitude and distance records, at one time holding all three at the same time. She attempted in 1931 to become the first woman to make a solo transatlantic flight but crashed in New Jersey, injured but alive.

Amelia Earhart is welcomed home after completing the first transatlantic solo flight by a woman, from Newfoundland to Northern Ireland, in 15 hours and 18 minutes, on May 21, 1932.

Fourteen people had been killed attempting this flight in the year since Lindbergh's successful attempt, including three women. On May 20, 1932, Amelia Earhart set out on a solo flight from Newfoundland in her red Lockheed Vega, seeking to match Charles Lindbergh's 1927 feat. After nearly 15 hours, Earhart touched down safely in a farmer's pasture in County Derry, Northern Ireland, becoming the first woman and the second pilot in history to fly solo across the Atlantic. This time, Earhart knew her fame was earned.

Earhart didn't stop there. She also became the first woman to complete a transcontinental flight alone, nonstop. Then, in a new Vega 5C, she became the first solo pilot to fly from Hawaii to Oakland, Calif.

After flying a Lockheed aircraft for the first time, Charles Lindbergh asked Gerard Vultee to design a high-performance, low-wing monoplane for route-surveying in a variety of climates, 1930.

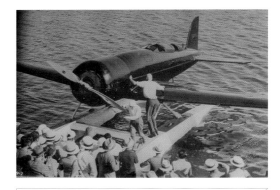

Charles Lindbergh's Sirius on the Yangtze River, China, 1931. While in Hankou, the British carrier HMS Hermes damaged the aircraft's fuselage and wings while attempting to store it. Lindbergh had the plane shipped back to California to be repaired by Lockheed. With the plane restored, Lindbergh continued to fly the Sirius through the 1930s to map new airline routes.

LINDBERGH'S LOCKHEED SIRIUS

Impressive as the Vega was, Charles Lindbergh needed something new to meet his next challenge: a scouting flight to Alaska, across the northern Pacific and on to China. He turned to Lockheed to invent the technology to meet his needs. Lindbergh's list of custom touches included a tandem cockpit with a sliding canopy to accommodate him and a copilot: his pregnant wife, Anne Morrow Lindbergh.

The fuselage needed to be big enough for state-of-the-art navigation equipment and a generator that could power the Lindberghs' electrically warmed flight suits. Lockheed Chief Engineer Gerard Vultee designed the Lockheed 8 Sirius, later given the name *Tingmissartoq* (Eskimo for "one that files like a big bird") based on Lindbergh's specifications. The Sirius was capable of traveling 185 miles per hour compared to the *St. Louis's* top speed of 133 mph. It was delivered in April 1930, and on the 20th of that month, the Lindberghs left Los Angeles and arrived in New York City 14 hours, 45 minutes and 32 seconds later — breaking the previous record by a full three hours.

Turning his sights toward Asia, Lindbergh sought more modifications. The Sirius was retrofitted as a sea plane, with pontoons in place of wheels. The engine was upgraded from 450hp to 575, and a new long-range radio was added to the communications equipment.

Lindbergh was greeted in China as a celebrity. But when his flights took him over areas of the Yangtze River struck by the worst flooding seen in decades, Lindbergh canceled his publicity functions and used the Sirius to deliver medicine and supplies to areas no one else could reach.

ONE-EYED WILEY

A former Oklahoma oilworker and reformed car thief, one-eyed pilot Wiley Post set out to complete an aerial circumnavigation of the globe. On June 23, 1931, Post took off with navigator Harold Gatty from Long Island's Roosevelt Field in his Vega 5B *Winnie Mae*. After battling sleeplessness, fatigue, bad weather and poor landing fields, they arrived home having set an around-the-world record. Two years later, Post beat his own record in the same *Winnie Mae*, this time flying solo with a Sperry autopilot system.

Following that triumph, Post found a new challenge: high-altitude flight. The lower density of high-altitude air made higher speeds possible, so Post devised an innovative pressurized suit — which prefigured those used for stratospheric and space travel in the coming decades — and went after altitude records of the day. His *Winnie Mae* could top 340 mph, a huge leap compared to the first Vega's top speed of 135 mph. Though all reports claim he reached 55,000 feet, breaking the altitude record, his measurement instruments failed, making the record unofficial.

Wiley Post, pictured here in 1935, set many records in his Vega *Winnie Mae*. From Los Angeles to Chicago (nine hours, nine minutes and four seconds, August 27, 1930); around the world (eight days, 15 hours, 51 minutes, June 23 to July 1, 1931); around the world (seven days, 18 hours, 49 minutes, July 15 to July 22, 1933).

The XP-900/YP-24 was the first Lockheed fighter, first U.S. military monoplane fighter and first U.S. military aircraft with fully retractable landing gear, 1931.

Charles R. "C.R." Smith of American Airways, later American Airlines, takes delivery of a Lockheed Orion from Lloyd Stearman, president of Lockheed Aircraft Company, 1932.

Static test on wing of the Orion using sandbags to simulate aerodynamic stress of flight, 1930.

HIGHS AND LOWS

All the record-setting feats of the early 1930s inspired the country to try air travel. Building off the success of the Vega and the Sirius, other models — the Air Express, Altair and Orion — made passenger transport a reality. Twelve U.S. airlines operated the Orion, a low-wing modification of the Vega, while other Orions, such as Jimmy Doolittle's Shellightning, were used as executive transport aircraft.

In spite of these successes, Lockheed could not overcome the effects of the Great Depression. With strong technological innovations but a weak balance sheet, it was forced into receivership, a type of corporate bankruptcy.

Allan Lockheed's attempts to launch new aircraft with Loughead Brothers Aircraft (and later with Alcor Aircraft Corporation) never got off the ground. Reeling from the financial turmoil of the Depression, Allan Lockheed resorted to working as a real estate salesman.

THE FLYING WHALE

Glenn Martin, too, felt the weight of the Depression by the early 1930s. His company recorded a loss of $46,145 in 1931, beginning a downturn that would extend into the mid-1930s. Still, he hoped for a turnaround and realized the company would have to look beyond military customers.

In 1931, Martin and his new chief engineer, Lessiter Milburn, began designing two new aircraft: a high-speed Army bomber for the military and a massive flying boat for commercial airlines.

When a prototype of Martin's new B-10 bomber lost a critical Army flying competition to a faster Boeing aircraft, Martin was devastated. On Milburn's insistence, Martin agreed to modify the aircraft, but because his doctor had mandated a restful vacation, Martin would not be a part of the effort. Milburn took over the urgent redesign. Martin engineers expanded the wings while adding more powerful twin engines and enlarging the fuselage, inspiring the nickname *The Flying Whale*.

By 1934, Henry H. Arnold was leading a flight of 10 B-10 bombers from Washington on a six-day mapping mission of the Arctic. Using Fairbanks, Alaska, as a base, Arnold's B-10s photographed more than 200,000 square miles of previously uncharted territory, including new air routes over Russia and the Arctic Circle. After the mission, Arnold called the plane "the air power wonder of its day."[8]

Sixteen Martin B-10Bs under construction. A total of 103 were built at the Middle River plant, and another two were built from spares, 1936.

THE B-10 WAS NO WHALE IN FLIGHT. IT WAS THE FASTEST BOMBER IN THE WORLD.

The moniker was deceptive. The B-10 was no whale in flight. It was the fastest bomber in the world, capable of outrunning every pursuit plane in America's arsenal. The aircraft's 2,000-pound internal bomb capacity, and the addition of the world's first enclosed rotating machine gun turret, made it as formidable as it was fast.

When the Martin Corporation's B-10 set its retractable landing gear down on Wright Field near Dayton, Ohio, in fall 1932, the Air Corps realized it had found its dream plane. The B-10 was America's first large all-metal monoplane, boasting a range of 1,400 miles and a top speed of 207 mph, 22 mph faster than its nearest competitor. The Army immediately ordered 14 B-10s, establishing the aircraft as the marquee bomber of its era.

The B-10 earned Glenn Martin the 1932 Collier Trophy, America's most distinguished aviation award, presented by President Franklin D. Roosevelt. The B-10 served in every bombardment group in the Army Air Corps during the 1930s, carrying out the Army's first test of the Norden precision bombsight in 1935, which helped bombardiers determine the exact moment a bomb should be dropped to hit a designated target. A year later, variants of the B-10 were exported overseas, eventually reaching a diverse range of nations. Martin sold more than 190 B-10s overseas, primarily to the Netherlands, but also to customers in Argentina and Turkey.

The B-10 was not the only Martin plane of the era to extend the company's reach overseas. In June 1931, the head of Pan American Airways, Juan Trippe, contacted Glenn Martin seeking bids for a long-range "flying boat" meant for both air mail and passenger transport. Martin overruled his military-focused engineering staff and went after the commercial contract. Trippe approved Martin's plans for three of these flying boats, but at a much lower price than Martin initially quoted. Though Martin's business manager said the contract would bankrupt the company, Glenn accepted the price. Although the famous *China Clipper* would become an international icon, it was a financial failure. The decision would nearly send the company into bankruptcy, and indeed, Martin lost money in its first seven years in Middle River.

U.S. military and foreign sales of the B-10 bomber reversed these fortunes beginning in 1936. As Martin's company engineered this turnaround, the bankrupt Lockheed operation soon received its own influx of new energy and financing.

PUSHING THE ENVELOPE

On the morning of June 21, 1932, a neatly dressed young Harvard grad stood in a U.S. district courtroom in Los Angeles holding a single white envelope. He had come to purchase the assets of the Lockheed Aircraft Corporation. When the judge asked if there were any bidders for the company, only the young man stepped forward, sliding the envelope onto the judge's bench. It contained an offer of $40,000, cobbled together from a consortium of investors.

The judge was blunt. "I hope, young man, you know what you're doing," he said.[9]

"I do," responded Lockheed's new buyer, who would walk out of the courtroom and spend the remainder of his life turning Lockheed into one of the most dynamic aerospace companies in the world.

His name was Robert E. Gross.

Gross was optimistic but realistic. Unlike his predecessors, he was not an aviator and had no engineering background. But Gross had previously purchased an interest in Stearman Aircraft and later formed the Viking Flying Boat Company with his brother Courtlandt. With his business acumen and ability to inspire employees, he would lead Lockheed from bankruptcy into the space race.

Robert E. Gross bought the bankrupt Lockheed operation for $40,000 and founded the new Lockheed company with Ronald King, Cyril Chappellet and Hall Hibbard, 1932.

Gross built a forward-thinking, financially stable company composed of talented employees and future leaders. His relationships with engineer-manufacturer Lloyd Stearman, "adventurer-businessman" Cyril Chappellet and his brother would bear fruit in the new, young operation.[10] He also had a great eye for talent, as evidenced by one of his first hires, engineer Hall Hibbard.

Gross's lack of engineering training was a foil to prod Lockheed's engineers, and he repeatedly encouraged them to risk failure in order to create seemingly impossible machines. The first of these instances came on a fall day in 1932, soon after Gross took over the company, as he sat in the coffee shop of the Union Air Terminal. Gross carefully observed as passengers boarded airliners on the ramps outside. Three planes were poised to depart: a single-engine Lockheed Orion, a Ford Trimotor and Boeing's Model 247, a twin-engine aircraft. Lockheed's founding Secretary Cyril Chappellet recalled:

Lockheed's corporate logo from 1932 until 1979.

Bob said to himself, "Now, as an uninterested flier of air transportation, which of these two planes would I prefer to entrust myself to?" … Bob decided that he and most people would prefer to buy a ticket on a multi-engine airplane. So he came back to the factory and told Hall [Hibbard] to scrap his drawings for the single-engine large plane and to start in on a small, twin-engine plane.[11]

Gross wanted an aircraft that embodied the very latest in engineering innovations, a plane that would be fast and inexpensive to produce, and easily adaptable to the constantly evolving aviation market. Rather than working with a single designer, as had been standard practice, he turned to a team of developers already in place — men such as noted engineers Richard Von Hake and Lloyd Stearman — who each had experience building their own planes. Hall Hibbard led the design team. Together, the Lockheed team created a unique prototype. It was called the Electra Model 10, named after a star in the Pleiades cluster.

Lockheed Aircraft Corporation executives in 1934 included (left to right) Assistant Treasurer Ronald King, Vice President-Sales Manager Carl B. Squier, President Lloyd Stearman, Robert Gross, Secretary Cyril Chappelet and Assistant Chief Engineer Hall Hibbard.

Engineering wunderkind Clarence "Kelly" Johnson in a University of Michigan wind tunnel with the early single-tail Model 10 Electra. Johnson's aerodynamic testing led to twin-tail design, later a Lockheed trademark, 1934.

THE WUNDERKIND

By 1933, the Electra development team also included a 23-year-old tool designer who had recently graduated from the University of Michigan's aerodynamics program. His name was Clarence Johnson, but ever since he'd trounced a local bully in grade school, he went by the more defiant nickname "Kelly," which suited his fierce and pugnacious personality. Shortly after he was hired, Johnson walked into his new boss's office, pointed to the Electra and isolated a critical instability. As a graduate student in Ann Arbor, Johnson had worked long hours conducting wind-tunnel tests for aircraft manufacturers, and Hibbard backed Johnson in his initial hunch. Hibbard sent Johnson back to Michigan, this time as a Lockheed employee, to run additional wind-tunnel tests on the Electra.

Electra wind-tunnel testing of additional fins near the end of the tailplane, 1941.

After more than 70 tests, Johnson pulled the model airplane out of the wind tunnel for the final time. Johnson's insight, confirmed by these tests, was that the Electra's single-tail configuration lacked stability. He recommended a twin-tail design, with the rudders placed directly behind each engine. Not only did the twin-tail version far outperform the initial Electra design, it became a signature of other Lockheed models.

Johnson's wind-tunnel work marked the first of many crucial insights and innovations that branded him the century's leading aircraft designer. It also represented the progressive approach to teamwork that Gross brought to Lockheed when he bought the company. In various configurations, thousands of Electras were sold around the world in the decade that followed, making it one of the most important airliners in a new era of commercial world travel.

FROM JUNIOR TO SUPER

The success of the Lockheed Electra was due in part to its flexibility. Sensing a larger market, Vice President of Sales Carl Squier compelled Hall Hibbard and Kelly Johnson to design both smaller and larger versions of the popular aircraft, which yielded the Model 12 Electra Junior and Model 14 Super Electra, respectively.

The smaller six-passenger Electra Junior — which reduced the original plane's wing area by 23 percent yet ensured a respectable top speed of 225 mph — was intended for smaller airlines, private owners and government agencies. Beginning in June 1936, it found a market at home and overseas. A total of 130 Model 12s were produced, with seven delivered to the U.S. Navy and 36 to the government of the Dutch East Indies. For private owners like James Sidney Cotton, a British World War I ace, the Electra Junior was the perfect plane, both fast and easily maneuverable. Cotton hid seven cameras on his personal aircraft and flew numerous missions in his Electra Junior above the Mediterranean and North Africa throughout 1939, snapping key photographs of Nazi positions. His work led to the formation of the Royal Air Force's Photographic Reconnaissance Unit, and in some ways served as a predecessor for future Lockheed spy planes and satellites.

The Electra's bigger cousin, the 14-passenger Model 14 Super Electra, caught the eye of a man who seemed determined to conquer the skies. The irrepressible Howard Hughes, a businessman, playboy and aviator known for his daring motion picture epics, set out in 1938 to achieve his most daunting goal yet: setting the speed record for an around-the-world flight. He asked Lockheed to equip a Super Electra with 1,100hp engines and the latest in radio and navigation equipment. The Electra proved more than up to the task, averaging 206 mph for Hughes, who flew around the world in just 71 hours, 11 minutes and 10 seconds.

Electra advertisement, 1936.

The *China Clipper* took Glenn L. Martin from Newport Beach to Avalon, Calif., to celebrate the 25th anniversary of his record flight in an early Martin sea plane, 1937.

The first of three M-130 *Clippers* built for Pan American Airways, 1934.

Passengers sit aboard the Electra 10, 1934.

By this time, Lockheed's Model 14 Super Electras were selling well, especially to overseas commercial carriers. Lockheed pitted its Super Electra against the Douglas DC-3, offering an aircraft that boasted a 45-mph speed advantage and new Fowler flaps, an innovation that increased wing area to reduce approach and landing speeds. By 1937, Lockheed had $5 million in orders for this regal Model 14, ultimately building 112 planes that could be seen taking off and landing at airports from Poland to Japan.

COMMERCIAL AIR TRAVEL

In October 1936, the Martin M-130 *Hawaii Clipper* brought passengers to the Philippines. Next, regular passenger service to Hong Kong began, with the *Philippine Clipper* spiriting 15 passengers there in three days' time. By boat, this 8,200-mile route would have taken three weeks.

A new era of air travel had arrived.

Kelly Johnson reviews data on the Electra Model 10E with Amelia Earhart, 1937.

The Electra, too, immediately attracted the interest of airlines, especially Northwest Airlines and Pan American Airways, which purchased Electras for their fleets by the end of 1934. But Gross knew he needed to attract private plane enthusiasts and the military if he wanted sales to outpace private development costs. Enter Amelia Earhart.

Like Wiley Post and countless others, Earhart set her sights on circumnavigating the globe. However, Earhart wanted to complete the trip along a grueling 9,000-mile route following the equator, the longest distance yet attempted. The aircraft she'd use for the journey would be a Lockheed Electra. To enable the plane to travel farther between fueling stops, Lockheed engineers equipped her 10-E Electra with special tanks that allowed the plane to carry 1,200 gallons of fuel instead of the customary 200. Earhart's mission was both unprecedented and dangerous.

Kelly Johnson collaborated with Amelia Earhart as she prepared for her flight around the world. Working closely with the aviator to develop new and complex flying protocols to extend the range of Earhart's plane, Johnson flew with Earhart as she prepared for her journey.

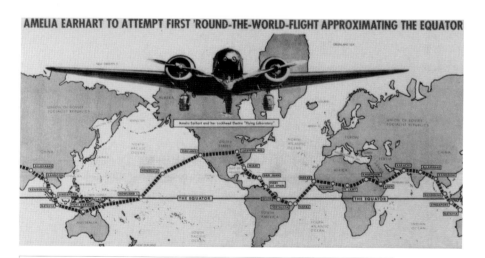

Amelia Earhart's proposed equatorial route around the world appeared in the New York Herald Tribune, 1937.

It became clear to those close to Earhart that she was not focused on the flight. She was supervising the construction of a new house, campaigning for President Roosevelt and endorsing her new luggage line. Before takeoff, she inexplicably left behind her Morse code key, a crucial piece of radio equipment, her parachute, her life raft and even her good-luck bracelet. After flying east through South America, Africa and Asia, Earhart and her navigator, Fred Noonan, departed for Howland Island, 2,500 miles east of New Guinea. After sporadic radio contact, they disappeared on July 2, 1937, somewhere over the South Pacific.

Similar tragedy had struck two years earlier when famed aviator Wiley Post, along with his friend and fellow Oklahoman, humorist Will Rogers, set off for Alaska. Post attempted too much customization for his chosen aircraft on this journey. Beginning with a modified Lockheed Orion and a wing from a Lockheed Explorer, he asked Lockheed engineers to install pontoons on the Orion-Explorer hybrid. Lockheed refused, claiming the pontoons would destroy the plane's aerodynamic integrity.

As it turns out, the company was correct. Post had the plane fitted with pontoons anyway, which made the aircraft nose-heavy, and on August 15, 1935, the plane stalled on takeoff near Point Barrow. Post and Rogers perished in the crash.

Wiley Post with his Orion-Explorer hybrid sea plane, which was built by mating the wing of Explorer 4 with an Orion 9E, 1935.

In June 1936, the War Department contracted with Lockheed to create a fast, high-altitude flier, the XC-35. During test flights, the plane reached a top speed of 350 mph, and the pressurized cabin made flight possible above 30,000 feet without the use of oxygen. The XC-35 earned the Collier Trophy for the most significant aircraft development of 1937.

WAR CLOUDS OVER EUROPE

As another European war appeared to be imminent, it became clear that aircraft would play a decisive role in future conflicts. Fighters and bombers such as those created by Glenn L. Martin were a key part of the U.S. defensive armament effort. Lockheed contributed to the military preparedness effort as well, notably with the XC-35, the world's first aircraft with a cabin that was pressurized for high altitudes. Hibbard and Johnson also began designing the P-38, one of the most innovative airborne weapons of the looming military conflict.

A ground crew hoists a 500-pound bomb onto an external rack of a Martin B-10B, with open bomb bay doors visible at right. The B-10B was capable of carrying 2,260 pounds of bombs, 1937.

CHAPTER 3

MASS PRODUCTION PLANTS

To Fill the Sky

1937–1945

"YOU CAME OUT TO CALIFORNIA, PUT ON YOUR PANTS, AND TOOK YOUR LUNCH PAIL TO A MAN'S JOB. THIS WAS THE BEGINNING OF WOMEN FEELING THAT THEY COULD BE SOMETHING MORE."[1]

—SYBIL LEWIS, RIVETER FOR LOCKHEED

A FACTORY TRANSFORMED

From the modest height of 5,000 feet, it looked like any sleepy California suburb. Single-family bungalows on gently sloping hills. Lawns inscribed with laundry lines and split-rail fences.

Descend lower and you would find a grand illusion perpetrated by artists, set designers and painters from nearby movie studios. By the early 1940s, Lockheed's Burbank plant was operating beneath a 1,000-acre canopy of chicken wire, netting and canvas painted to blend in with the grass.

Aerial photograph of Burbank factory camouflage, 1943. [INSET] Aerial photograph of the Burbank factory before the camouflage.

To protect against bombing raids, Disney studio technicians draped about 1,000 acres of canvas and chicken wire across buildings and parking lots, which were also dotted with wire, feather trees and burlap houses to give the factory the look of a suburb from the air, 1943.

Employees attending an awards ceremony beneath their Operation Camouflage netting, 1944.

Fake trees were covered with leaves made of chicken feathers. Airfields and parking lots were painted green to look like alfalfa fields. Operation Camouflage was in full effect — and not just in Burbank. On the East Coast, Martin's Middle River plant was undergoing a similar cloaking.

The aerial disguise — put into place to hide American aircraft factories from enemy eyes — was hardly the only major transformation at Lockheed during the World War II years. Under this massive tent, some 94,000 employees traversed an elaborate system of underground walkways, passing newly installed bomb shelters and huge anti-aircraft guns. But amid all these cosmetic and structural alterations, the most striking change was the workforce itself.

Before World War II, only five Lockheed employees were women. By June 1943, that number had exploded to nearly 35,000. Women and African Americans did their part to defend the country and proved their worth in the workplace.

The workforce of the Glenn L. Martin Company underwent a similar shift. On October 20, 1941, an initial group of 19 women punched the clock at Martin's Nebraska plant. Six months later, after America's entry into the war, more than 2,000 women were working in Martin's Omaha and Baltimore factories. When aircraft industry employment peaked at 2.1 million workers in November 1943, women accounted for 37 percent of this labor force. "Rosie the Riveter" had become an American icon.

The wartime years broke gender and racial barriers in service of a revolutionary effort to expand aircraft production on an unprecedented scale. Thousands of fighter, bomber, transport and reconnaissance planes produced by Lockheed, Martin, and heritage companies Consolidated and Vultee during World War II served a vital need in a conflict that could be won or lost in the air.

Martin workers on a power turret assembly line. Like most wartime suppliers, Martin recruited women and African American workers for production jobs, 1944.

Glenn L. Martin with his mother, Minta, during Hero Day at the Middle River plant, August 26, 1943.

The XPBM-1 (Model 162) Mariner prototype. The horizontal tail was changed to the upswept pinwheel tail after flight testing. More than 1,300 of the patrol bombers were built in several variants for the U.S. Navy, 1939.

EUROPE IN CRISIS

In September 1938, British Prime Minister Neville Chamberlain flew in his Lockheed Electra to a historic conference in Munich, joining French Premier Edouard Daladier and Italian dictator Benito Mussolini. Adolf Hitler, who had controlled Germany since 1933, hosted the conference. In the months before Munich, Hitler invaded Austria and Czechoslovakia, and Prime Minister Chamberlain hoped an appeasement strategy — allowing Hitler to keep his conquered territories — might achieve "peace with honor" and effectively end the Nazi quest for global domination.

While the United States maintained its political distance, American aircraft manufacturers like Glenn Martin saw the world with clear eyes. In 1938, Martin and his mother, Minta, toured Europe — visiting Germany and Italy as well as England, France, Holland and Switzerland. Martin made official reports to U.S. leaders and suggested the United States immediately ramp up production of long-range bombers, which he felt would be key in the inevitable conflict. His advice fell on deaf ears, with a Congressional committee insisting that the American strategy was one of short-range defense.

Regardless of the United States' attitude, Martin's resolve was undiminished. He returned to Middle River and redoubled the company's efforts to produce a prototype for what would soon become the U.S. Navy's largest, heaviest and longest-range patrol bomber — the PBM Mariner.

In the meantime, Great Britain was already seeking help from leaders of the global aviation industry.

OLD BOOMERANG

With news of Hitler's recent annexation of Austria sending shockwaves across Europe in April 1938, a contingent of the British Air Commission led by Sir Henry Self landed in New York on a vital mission. European airplane manufacturers were operating at near capacity. Self's team urgently needed to survey manufacturing facilities in the United States and find novel ideas for warplanes.

The Lockheed Aircraft Corporation presented the commission with a full-sized wooden mockup of what designer Kelly Johnson called a "convertible transport bomber." By modifying Lockheed's Super Electra with a bomb bay and three machine guns, Johnson designed the first American aircraft to destroy an enemy aircraft during World War II: the Hudson.

Courtlandt S. Gross, president of Lockheed subsidiary Vega Aircraft Corp., 1942.

The Hudson bomber was part of a new class of military aircraft used in World War II, 1940.

British war poster of Hudson with British Coastal Command, 1942.

Lockheed, at the time inexperienced in manufacturing military aircraft, was committed to earning the trust of the Royal Air Force. Johnson and Courtlandt Gross, now a central part of Lockheed's management team, traveled to London to finalize the sale of the new Hudson bomber, but the British Air Ministry requested numerous design changes. The 28-year-old Johnson sprang into action, even though it meant a few sleepless nights.

> When I finally fell into bed for some very sound sleep — in the room I shared with Courtlandt to save on expenses — it was the first time I had removed my clothes in 72 hours. I awoke the next morning to discover that [Courtlandt] had had my suit pressed and my shoes shined. How wonderful, I thought, that the head of the company would do something like that for an employee.[2]

After the Herculean effort to integrate all the suggested changes, Lockheed produced an entirely new plywood model, complete in every detail right down to a choice of alternate nose designs. In a matter of just a few days, Lockheed had given the British the aircraft they desired.

The contract, signed on June 23, 1938, authorized Lockheed to produce up to 250 Hudson bombers by December 1939, making it the largest contract to date for an international airplane sale by an American company. Competitors doubted Lockheed would meet its deadline, but Sir Arthur Harris, who would later lead the RAF's Bomber Command, felt differently. "I was entirely convinced that anyone who could produce a mock-up in twenty-four hours would indeed make good on all his promises — and this Lockheed most certainly did," he wrote.[3] The company established manufacturing facilities and support bases in Liverpool and Ireland, the latter responsible for assembling, modifying and repairing some 22,500 aircraft of all types during Britain's greatest time of need.

The Hudson bomber — nicknamed *Old Boomerang* because of its ability to withstand enemy fire and safely return home — earned innumerable accolades during the war. It primarily served with the RAF Coastal Command hunting German and Japanese submarines, but Hudson crews also provided convoy escort, participated in the RAF's first thousand-aircraft raid into Germany, performed reconnaissance missions and dropped spies behind enemy lines.

THE *SPIRIT OF LOCKHEED-VEGA EMPLOYEES*

One December morning in 1940, a 21-year-old night-shift workman from the Lockheed subsidiary Vega Aircraft Corp. named Burton Griffin found himself tossing and turning in bed, unable to shake an exciting idea that had taken hold in his imagination. He'd just come from working on the line at the company's plant in Burbank, Calif., helping to produce the much-needed Hudson bombers on order from Great Britain.

Playing a role in producing the bombers wasn't enough for Griffin, however. He wanted to persuade his fellow workers to volunteer their time or money to build a special employee-donated Hudson, which he believed would be the perfect Christmas gift to the imperiled people of Britain.

Each Hudson bomber cost $90,000 and demanded 24,000 employee hours to build. Assembling the gift in three weeks' time would be no easy task. But Lockheed-Vega executives embraced the idea. And after Griffin's plan was circulated, nearly all of his 20,000 colleagues — who earned 75 cents an

hour — agreed to donate two or more hours of pay toward the effort.

By December 25, the special Hudson, inscribed with the moniker the *Spirit of Lockheed-Vega Employees*, flew from California to St. Hubert Airport in Montreal, where it was handed over to British forces. A week later, upon its arrival in Great Britain, Lord Beaverbrook, the minister of aircraft in Britain, called the gift, "a message of immense encouragement"[4] and swiftly put it into service under the RAF's Coastal Command.

On August 27, 1941, as part of the RAF's No. 269 Squadron, the *Spirit* joined other Hudsons in being the first aircraft to capture a German submarine. The plane was subsequently damaged beyond repair during a ground accident in North Africa in July 1943, but not before making the employees of Lockheed-Vega, and its adoptive country, proud of its wartime efforts.

Donated by the workers at Lockheed to the RAF, the *Spirit of Lockheed-Vega Employees* is painted prior to its final shipment from Burbank, Calif., 1940.

Vega Plant 1, B-17 wing subassembly line, 1942.

The Engineering Department at one of Lockheed's plants during World War II, 1940.

Employees enter the Burbank plant during shift change, 1942.

THE BLITZ BEGINS

On September 1, 1939, German troops, tanks and about 2,000 aircraft attacked Poland — a country under British and French protection — sparking the start of World War II. By the end of 1940, Hitler's vicious and unflinching blitzkrieg campaign had overpowered Norway, Denmark, Luxembourg, Belgium, the Netherlands and France.

Only Great Britain had the firepower and technology to prevent Hitler's complete control of Europe.

To make good on the Hudson bomber contract, Lockheed's workforce had swelled from 7,000 in 1939 to almost 17,000 in 1940. After President Franklin D. Roosevelt called for massive expansion of the air force in a May 1940 speech, the drumbeat of war resounded at both Lockheed and Martin, spurring innovation in aircraft design and production processes for both companies.

After the Hudson bomber, Lockheed was selected to design and build the iconic P-38 Lightning. The Lockheed-Vega subsidiary, meanwhile, contributed heavily to the mass production effort on the Boeing B-17 Flying Fortress, building 2,250 of the nearly 13,000 B-17s made during World War II.

Glenn Martin's company also grew exponentially, following the first production of PBM-1 Mariners with new attack bombers, Martin models 167 and 187, as well as the B-26 Marauder.

Consolidated Aircraft, a Lockheed heritage company, also made major contributions to the war effort, building more than 18,000 Consolidated B-24 Liberator bombers — the most-produced American military aircraft of all time — as well as PBY Catalina patrol bombers that would play a pivotal role in antisubmarine warfare.

Two RAF Martin Model 167 Maryland IIs in North Africa. Great Britain's RAF purchased 150 Maryland IIs, in addition to operating 85 ex-French 167-A3s as Maryland Is, 1941.

The Martin Model 187 Baltimore, the first Baltimore I attack bomber in flight, 1941. The RAF bought 1,575 aircraft in the Baltimore series. The only Martin aircraft produced in greater numbers was the B-26 Marauder.

MARTIN B-26 MARAUDER

The B-26 Marauder is one of the most recognizable planes produced by the Glenn L. Martin Company. Designed by 27-year-old project engineer Peyton M. Magruder, the plane met specifications outlined by the Army Air Corps for a new medium bomber. The Martin design, Model 179, incorporated many advanced design features — including an aerodynamic fuselage, self-sealing fuel tanks and a powered gun turret. In August 1939, a few weeks before fighting broke out in Europe, the Model 179 was chosen as the winner of the Army contract.

Originally contracted to produce 201 planes, Martin received an order for an additional 930 before the B-26 had even flown, funded through President Roosevelt's "50,000-plane" program. November 25, 1940, marked the first flight of the B-26, and after reviewing the performance of the aircraft, the British placed an order for 459 additional planes. By 1945, when production ended, 5,266 Marauders had been built, with U.S., British, Free French, Australian, South African and Canadian aircrews all having flown the B-26 in combat.

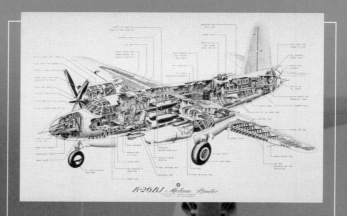

A cutaway drawing of a B-26B Series 10 Marauder (drawing is mislabeled B-26B1) showing some of the changes made to later production B-26Bs, such as the twin nose and tail guns and the forward-firing package guns just aft and below the cockpit, 1943.

A formation of B-26F-1 Marauders over France, 1944.

LOCKHEED P-38 LIGHTNING

First conceived in 1937 by Lockheed chief engineer Hall L. Hibbard and then-assistant Kelly Johnson, the twin-boomed P-38 was the most innovative fighter plane of its day, combining speed with unheard-of advances: two supercharged engines and a potent mix of four .50-caliber machine guns and a 20 mm cannon. The P-38 was capable of climbing to 3,300 feet in a single minute and reaching 400 mph. It also doubled as an intimidating long-range threat, capable of carrying a substantial payload and boasting a range of 1,150 miles.

In 1937, the Army Air Corps authorized building the prototype XP-38, which was delivered on January 1, 1939. The prototype's first flight took place January 27, 1939, and the first service models were delivered in June 1941. The P-38 primarily served in Europe and North Africa although its long range and twin engines made it well suited for duty in the Pacific theater, as well.

Although effective as a dive bomber, long-range escort and reconnaissance plane, the P-38's legacy as a fighter plane is unmatched. More than 10,000 P-38s — including 18 distinct models — were manufactured during the war, flying more than 130,000 missions around the world. P-38s also shot down more Japanese aircraft than any other Army Air Corps fighter, with America's leading aerial ace, Maj. Richard Bong, scoring 40 victories in the P-38.

P-38 machine gun firing test, with .50-caliber machine guns firing a tracer with every fifth shell, 1941.

Major Richard Bong with his personal P-38 Lightning, *Marge*, named after his wife, in 1944.

P-38 Lightnings in formation with an F-5, the photoreconnaissance version of the Lightning 1940. The F-5 obtained 90 percent of the aerial film captured over Europe during the war.

CONSOLIDATED PBY CATALINA AND B-24 LIBERATOR

Protecting transport vessels and warships from German U-boat attacks was as great a challenge in World War II as it had been in World War I. Beginning in 1936, the U.S. Navy depended on the Consolidated PBY Catalina antisubmarine patrol aircraft, and supplied the RAF Coastal Command with large numbers of these workhorse planes, as well. The first "Cat" flew on March 28, 1935, and more than 4,000 were produced overall, more than any other flying boat in history.

Later models of the twin-engine, parasol-mounted sea plane also featured retractable tricycle landing gear. In addition to saving hundreds of downed pilots, Catalinas also proved hugely valuable in long-range reconnaissance patrols, playing crucial roles in battles in the European and Pacific theaters.

When American aircraft manufacturers nationwide were supplementing production of B-17s, Consolidated was also offered a contract to help build the iconic bomber. Instead, Consolidated founder Reuben Fleet offered to design a different four-engine bomber to complement the B-17.

Conceived in 1938, the B-24 prototype was designed to fly faster and carry a larger payload than the Army's B-17 Flying Fortress. In time, the B-24 would boast a long, tapered wing atop its fuselage, which allowed impressive long-range cruising capabilities. A B-24 could reach a top speed of 290 mph and carry a 5,000-pound bomb load for 1,700 miles.

By 1941, the B-24 was being shipped to Great Britain. It was dubbed the Liberator and adapted for a variety of purposes. The Liberator's range proved invaluable in coastal scouting and hunting German U-boats, creating safe passage for Allied transports and destroyers headed for Europe. It also bombed German-controlled oil fields and attacked critical targets in Italy, turning the tide in the Allies' Mediterranean campaign. All told, more Liberators were built than any other American aircraft in World War II, a tremendous distinction.

A Royal Australian Air Force PBY-2 Catalina aircraft in flight. This aircraft was first delivered to the RAAF on June 1, 1945.

IN THE RING

On December 7, 1941, as word of the Japanese attack on Pearl Harbor reached California, some 53,000 Lockheed employees in 150 Southern California communities stepped outside their homes to watch as countless P-38 fighters and Hudson bombers streaked across the sky. After Pearl Harbor, all battle-ready aircraft were ordered into the air. Some flew west to protect the nation against another potential Japanese attack. Others were guided inland to protect against strafing runs. And still others simply patrolled the skies to give the nation a sense of security in a time of crisis.

The Lockheed P-38 Lightning would soon see action in Europe and North Africa against the Luftwaffe and in the Pacific theater against the Japanese. Meanwhile, Martin aircraft began entering operational service around the globe: Martin 167 and M-167F Marylands were flown by Free French and British pilots in North Africa, while early Martin 187 Baltimores and Marauders were also delivered to the British. B-10s began flying in the Philippines and Java while PBMs saw service in the Atlantic.

With American men in combat as of December 1941, the key labor question was how quickly women could be trained to work on assembly lines.

Newspapers across the country carried the story of 60 Pearl Harbor widows who responded to job offers at the Lockheed and Lockheed-Vega plants in Burbank, Calif.,

Wartime production needs drew women of all backgrounds into the workforce, 1942.

A Martin employee works on the nose section of a B-26 Marauder at the company's Middle River plant, 1943.

"BIG AIRPLANES ARE MADE UP OF SMALL PARTS, AND WOMEN BUILD SMALL PARTS TO PERFECTION."

—COURTLANDT GROSS

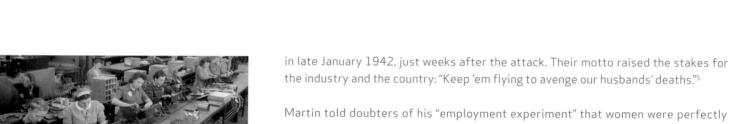

Lockheed factory floor space increased from its prewar 550,000 square feet to 7.7 million square feet in 1943.

in late January 1942, just weeks after the attack. Their motto raised the stakes for the industry and the country: "Keep 'em flying to avenge our husbands' deaths."[5]

Martin told doubters of his "employment experiment" that women were perfectly suited to handle most of the 25,000 parts that comprised a B-26. "Big airplanes are made up of small parts," Courtlandt Gross concurred, "and women build small parts to perfection."[6]

As the aircraft industry sought to match (and later outperform) the mass production standards of auto assembly lines, additional hydraulic lifts, smaller rivet guns and other reengineered tools quickly put women on an equal footing with their male counterparts.

Ever-escalating demand for wartime labor opened factory doors to women of all backgrounds. Housewives and women fresh out of high school were sent into newly created training courses to learn the basics of riveting — often the first job offered to women. Day care centers were built adjacent to many factories so women with small children could join the war effort. Lockheed opened manufacturing satellites in Santa Barbara, Bakersfield and Fresno in part to attract suburban women who weren't accustomed to traveling into the city. Jobs at Lockheed and Martin gave a generation of women a fresh sense of accomplishment.

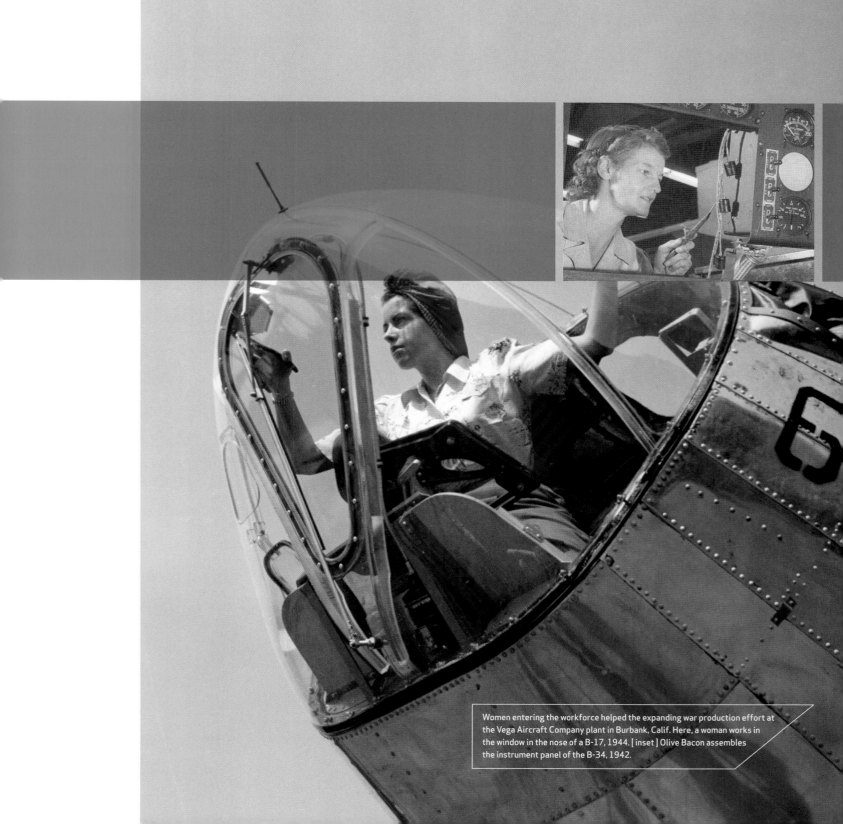

Women entering the workforce helped the expanding war production effort at the Vega Aircraft Company plant in Burbank, Calif. Here, a woman works in the window in the nose of a B-17, 1944. [inset] Olive Bacon assembles the instrument panel of the B-34, 1942.

ROSIE THE ENGINEER

While plenty of factory-floor Rosies were identified by the eager press, manufacturing jobs weren't the only positions filled by women. The ranks of college-educated engineers were depleted as men were called to active service.

The Advanced Development Group of Radio Corporation of America (RCA), a Lockheed Martin heritage company known today as the Advanced Technology Laboratories, participated in a groundbreaking solution to the problem. It sent off a group of promising women for intensive training at Purdue University in West Lafayette, Ind. Other industry leaders, notably Curtiss-Wright, did the same.

The first group of RCA Engineering Cadettes, with 86 women from 17 states, started classes on Purdue's campus in 1943, initiating 44 weeks of intense training in mathematics, drafting, carpentry, electrical circuit theory, electronics and radio theory. In February 1944, the first graduating class immediately began working as engineering aides in RCA Victor plants around the country. By war's end, 137 women had matriculated and gone to work for RCA.

While women held riveting and other manufacturing jobs during World War II, they also worked alongside men in the engineering department, creating highly technical drawings for the new fighters and bombers.

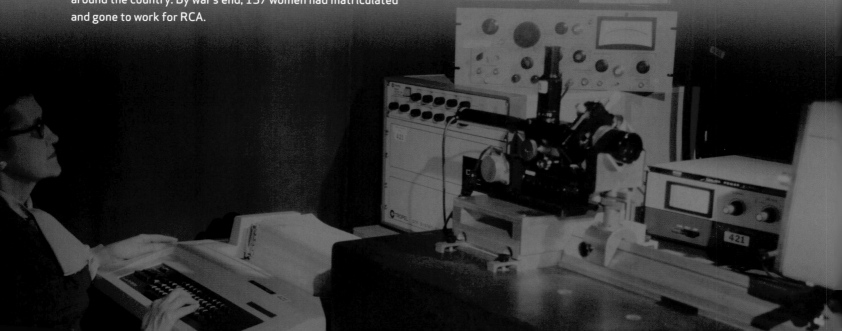

TRIAL BY FIRE

To win the war in the air, Allied aircraft had to succeed in multiple roles and in multiple theaters of combat. Naval patrol bombers like the PBM Mariner and PBY Catalina had to spot and sink enemy ships and submarines. Fighter planes like the P-38 had to outmaneuver and outgun their opponents. Bombers like the Hudsons, B-26 Marauders and B-24 Liberators had to hit strategic targets and return safely. The challenge was beyond all measure.

After America entered combat, one of the first of these challenges arrived on August 14, 1942, when the P-38 Lightning peeled down from the skies off the coast of Iceland. The aircraft's target, a German Focke-Wulf FW-200 patrol plane, had never encountered anything quite like it before. True to its name, the Lightning was a force of nature: fast, unforeseen and immensely powerful. The P-38 dispatched the Condor in seconds, marking the first successful American engagement of a German aircraft during World War II.

The "fork-tailed devil" in flight, 1944.

The P-38 showed its versatility in North Africa in November 1942, when a lone German pilot surrendered to soldiers at an Allied camp near Tunisia, pointing up to the sky and repeating the same hysterical phrase — "der Gableschwanz Teufl." The P-38 had been given a new nickname: the "fork-tailed devil."

In 1943, when code breakers learned of a key inspection flight in the Pacific by Japanese Admiral Isoroku Yamamoto, architect of the Pearl Harbor bombing, 16 P-38s were dispatched. It proved to be a turning point in the war. Embarking on what was at the time the longest intercept in history, the fleet shot down the admiral's bomber and his squadron of Mitsubishi A6M Zeros. Japanese naval morale was crushed.

Army students get firsthand knowledge of the P-38 at the Lockheed Service School, 1944.

Famed aviator Charles Lindbergh offered his services as a P-38 flight consultant. Flying missions with the 475th Airborne in 1944, he taught P-38 pilots techniques that stretched flight time from six hours to nine. On July 28, Lindbergh encountered a Mitsubishi Sonia, piloted by a veteran Japanese commander. The American civilian pilot, who had never engaged in open combat before, shot down the Sonia with his P-38.

"WE, THE MEN AND WOMEN WHO HELPED BUILD THIS AIRPLANE, WERE EVER MINDFUL THAT YOUR LIVES AND POSSIBLY OUR FUTURES MIGHT DEPEND ON HOW WELL WE DID OUR JOBS. WE, THEREFORE, PLEDGE THAT EVERY DETAIL OF CONSTRUCTION OF THE AIRPLANE WAS COMPLETED AS CAREFULLY AND THOROUGHLY AS THOUGH WE WERE TO FLY IT OURSELVES."[7]

— 1944 MARTIN EMPLOYEE PLEDGE, REGARDING THE B-26

During World War II, Martin became the world's largest manufacturer of power-operated aircraft turrets. More than 40,000 250CEs were built and used on a dozen different models of American and Allied aircraft, 1944.

STRATEGIC BOMBING

In comparison to the P-38, the B-26 Marauder had tougher growing pains. Because it was rushed from the drawing board to the production line, early problems surfaced, resulting in several training accidents that inspired the plane's nickname, "the widow maker," among other more colorful monikers. In response to these early problems, the plane was modified with longer wings and taller rudders. Golden Age aviator Jimmy Doolittle was called in to demonstrate the Marauder to future pilots.

The Marauder was initially deployed to the Pacific, but long takeoff and landing distances hampered its effectiveness. Bomber groups were shifted to North Africa, where the B-26 eventually experienced greater success. Early missions in Europe, however, did not go well. A mission to knock out a power station in Ijmuiden, Holland, ended in disaster, with 10 bombers lost and one aborted. War planners in Europe soon ordered a halt to the low-level bombing missions that had been effective in the Pacific. Far fewer B-26 losses occurred once the strategy shifted to higher-altitude runs.

On Hero Day at the Middle River plant, three B-26B Marauders visit the factory. Aircrews, Army brass and Glenn Martin address the workers to urge war bond sales, August 26, 1943.

Jimmy Doolittle and Peyton Magruder stand in front of the B-26 Marauder, 1943. Magruder designed the aircraft according to Army Air Corps specifications, and his proposal earned the highest rating of all the submitted designs. Between the two world wars, Doolittle worked for Shell Oil, persuading them to develop 100-octane aviation fuel, which became hugely important for the high-performance engines of the coming generation.

With the B-26 operating much more effectively, the Consolidated B-24 Liberator posted many of its own strategic bombing successes. On February 24, 1943, three squadrons of B-24 Liberators streaked toward Germany to hit the Luftwaffe at its heart, targeting a key production facility in the town of Gotha. Just a month earlier, B-24s had participated in the first attack on German soil, bombing a submarine yard in Wilhelmshaven. What awaited the Liberators over Gotha would be the ultimate test of the bomber's abilities.

Eighty minutes into their flight, German fighters swooped in to intercept the B-24 squadrons. Then came a firestorm of antiaircraft cannon shells and air-burst bombs, turning the skies into a hellish expanse of bullets, smoke and flak. Some B-24s fell and others limped back to England, but those who survived the onslaught dropped 98 percent of their bombs on target, leveling Gotha's aircraft factory in one amazing run.

A formation of B-26B Marauder medium bombers in flight, 1944.

A Consolidated B-24 Liberator releases its payload on a German rail yard, March 1945.

Two B-26 Marauders escort a damaged third Marauder (leaking fuel) back from a mission over France.

Camouflaged and natural metal B-26B and B-26F aircraft fly in formation over France in late summer 1944, wearing the invasion stripes painted on the undersides of all Allied aircraft for D-Day, 1944.

Considered one of the best examples of precision bombing in the war, the raid on Gotha hobbled German aircraft production and established the B-24 as one of the Allies' most trusted bombers. An August 1943 B-24 raid against the German oil refineries at Ploesti, Romania, was also critical. By June 6, 1944, B-24s found themselves at the heart of the D-Day invasion, softening Nazi positions before ground forces stormed the Normandy beaches.

THE TIDE TURNS

In late July and early August 1943, a campaign of air raids known as Operation Gomorrah, or "Blitz Week," saw the Allies employ blitzkrieg tactics similar to those of the Germans. The momentum was shifting in Europe, creating conditions for an Allied landing in Normandy on June 6, 1944 — D-Day — while Allied aircraft continued to intercept the German reserves. Within weeks, the Allies had advanced through France and stood on Germany's doorstep.

The Allies countered a final German offensive in the spring of 1945 by pounding Dresden with aerial raids and, with help from the advancing Soviet forces, succeeded in surrounding Berlin. Germany formally surrendered, ending the war in Europe on May 8, 1945. But the bloody battle in the Pacific dragged on.

While the apparent German collapse might have signaled the end of the war, separate technological races were playing out behind the scenes of this aerial, naval and ground war: namely, the advent of jet propulsion technology in both manned aircraft and unmanned aerial weapons — and, far more frightening, the race for an atomic weapon.

The Manhattan Project's advances in nuclear technology created the world's first atomic weapon and ultimately brought the war to an end. But it came at a terrible cost.

The Martin Company's Omaha, Neb., plant manufactured 536 Boeing B-29 Superfortress bombers during the war. In the summer of 1944, the U.S. government commissioned the plant to create a small number of modified B-29s, each capable

Martin employees in Omaha, Neb., factory with B-29. The government-owned Martin Nebraska plant built 536 B-29s after B-26C production ended at 1210, 1944.

A B-29 Superfortress under construction at the Martin Company's Omaha, Neb., plant, 1944.

of carrying a single 9,000-pound bomb. Two of those B-29s were the *Enola Gay* and the *Bockscar*.

On Aug. 6, 1945, a crew piloting the *Enola Gay* dropped an atomic weapon on the Japanese city of Hiroshima. When the Japanese still refused to surrender, a second crew flying the B-29 *Bockscar* dropped a second atomic weapon on Nagasaki.

On September 2, 1945, Japan formally surrendered. World War II was over.

A German civilian looks at a painting of Stalin on the Unter den Linden in Berlin, June 1945.

THE AFTERMATH

The reconstruction effort commenced and soldiers returned home. Most women left their factory jobs, but their role in supporting the war effort and the advancement of women in the workplace was not forgotten.

As the war ended, so did the service life of many of its aircraft. The Air Force took B-26s out of service, removing them all by the end of 1948. Some Hudson bombers stayed in service after the war as civilian transport aircraft serving Australia and New Zealand, but the more modern Lockheed Ventura replaced the Hudson in combat in late World War II. Consolidated's B-24 Liberators and PBY Catalinas were also retired by the 1950s. The P-38 was the only American pursuit plane to remain in constant production throughout World War II.

Although the war was over, relations between the Russians and their Western allies were fragile. Soviet dictator Joseph Stalin negotiated certain territory to remain under his nation's control, a "buffer zone" soon known as the Iron Curtain. By 1948, seven Eastern European countries were led by communist governments, and a new superpower had risen: the Soviet Union.

Lockheed Air Terminal employees pose with the last Hudson bomber produced, 1943.

CHAPTER 4

COVERT FACILITIES

Developing Deterrents

1946-1957

"FOR SOME TIME I HAD BEEN PESTERING GROSS
AND HIBBARD TO LET ME SET UP AN EXPERIMENTAL
DEPARTMENT WHERE THE DESIGNERS AND SHOP
ARTISANS COULD WORK TOGETHER CLOSELY. ...
THIS BECAME THE FIRST 'SKUNK WORKS.'"[1]

—KELLY JOHNSON

TOP SECRET

Kelly Johnson's elite team of engineers and mechanics gathered in 1943 in their makeshift facility at the edge of Lockheed's Burbank plant. With sturdy wood repurposed from Wright engine packing crates, they constructed the walls of a production area. A rented circus tent became their roof. Their top-secret mission: Design and build a prototype of what would become the United States' first operational jet fighter in a seemingly impossible 180 days. The team accepted the challenge, and soon created the XP-80, nicknamed *Lulu Belle*, the first in an unparalleled line of revolutionary aircraft to emerge from the so-called "Skunk Works" covert facility.

Donald Palmer and A.M. Viereck, project designers, with Kelly Johnson and the XP-80A prototype. With its bullet-shaped fuselage, flush rivets and smooth skin, the production P-80 was not only a looker but also an intimidating attack plane, boasting six .50-caliber machine guns and underwing bomb racks. [INSET] Building 82, Lockheed Skunk Works, 1957.

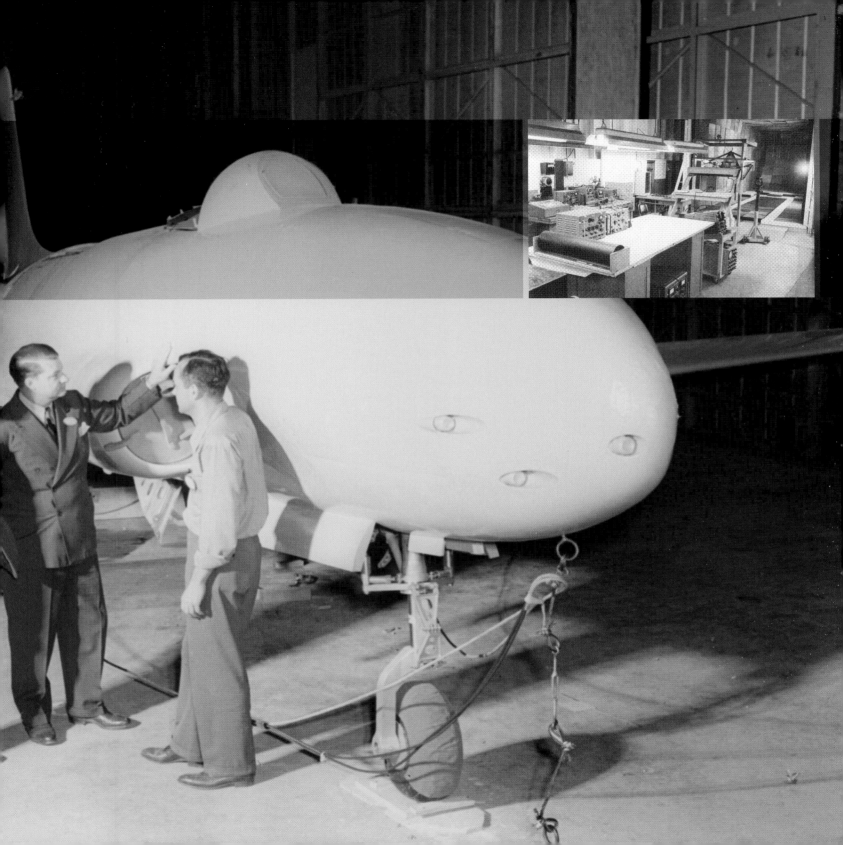

Production line at Skunk Works for the TF-80 operational trainer, 1948.

Six years after the first flight of the P-80, a fleet of Lockheed Shooting Stars raced high above North Korea's Yalu River. Twenty-five-year-old pilot Lt. Russell J. Brown pulled into firing position behind a Chinese MiG-15 and followed its dive toward Earth. Brown fired four short bursts from his .50-caliber guns, and once he saw smoke pouring from the MiG's fuselage, he went for the strike. The date was November 8, 1950, and the young pilot had just won the world's first jet-versus-jet dogfight. Hurtling down at 600 miles per hour, he quickly pulled out of his dive.

Two weeks later, on the other side of the world, a different sort of countdown hit zero. On New Mexico's vast Tularosa Basin — a flat expanse of desert protected by mountains standing like ancient sentries — the Martin Viking 5 sounding rocket lifted off from Launch Complex 33. The first iteration of the rocket, Viking 1, had reached the edge of "space" — defined in the United States as anything higher than 50 miles (80 kilometers) above sea level and internationally as 62 miles (100 kilometers) —

on May 3, 1949, while carrying 464 pounds of scientific instruments. When Viking 5 reached its zenith 108 miles over White Sands Proving Ground, Martin had demonstrated yet again that the dreams of countless stargazers could soon become a reality. The bonds of gravity could be broken. Travel to the stars was possible.

Post-World War II, secret technological races pushed aviation to unprecedented heights. Jet propulsion came of age during the Korean War, while mutual distrust between the United States and Soviet Union led to breakthroughs in rocketry. These aerial wonders paved the way for human space exploration, but as the two superpowers kept pace in their development of military capabilities — including manned and unmanned aerial weapons as well as reconnaissance aircraft — the Cold War soon defined the new global landscape.

EXPANSION AND CONTAINMENT

Postwar Soviet expansion hinged on the spread of an ideology — namely, communism. New regimes in Southeast Asia joined those already established in Eastern Europe when Russian troops liberated Korea from its longtime Japanese rulers in August 1945 and installed communist leadership in the North. But the imperialistic tendencies of Stalin's Soviet Union, and the tactics and strategies they would employ, were markedly different than those of Hitler's Germany.

In February 1946, U.S. diplomat George F. Kennan drew on his years of experience in Russia and drafted the so-called "Long Telegram" to the State Department. The memo outlined his views on Soviet expansion and, in turn, suggested a policy of U.S. containment. Kennan wrote:

> Soviet power, unlike that of Hitlerite Germany, is neither schematic nor adventuristic. ... For this reason it can easily withdraw — and usually does — when strong resistance is encountered at any point. Thus, if the adversary has sufficient force and makes clear his readiness to use it, he rarely has to do so. If situations are properly handled there need be no prestige-engaging showdowns.[2]

U.S. leaders largely adopted Kennan's suggestions as the core of their postwar Soviet strategy. From the beginning, the endgame was not to overpower the Soviets

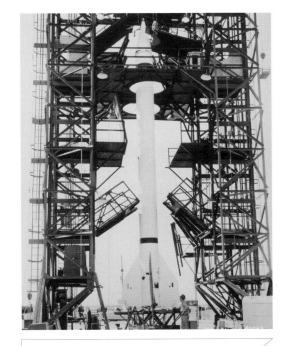

Viking 1 sounding rocket prepared for launch at White Sands Proving Ground, May 3, 1949.

"FROM VARIOUS SYMPTOMS ONE CAN INFER THAT THE RUSSIANS DO NOT YET POSSESS THE SECRET OF MAKING THE ATOMIC BOMB; ON THE OTHER HAND, THE CONSENSUS OF OPINION SEEMS TO BE THAT THEY WILL POSSESS IT WITHIN A FEW YEARS."[3]

—GEORGE ORWELL, "YOU AND THE ATOMIC BOMB," OCTOBER 1945

Kelly Johnson, head of Lockheed's Advanced Development Projects division, 1940.

in all-out battle, but to intentionally engineer a stalemate whereby both countries could save face and avoid bloodshed. Key components of this strategy would initially include the development of:

- A next-generation air force employing jet technology
- A sizeable arsenal of rockets and missiles capable of reaching overseas
- Effective reconnaissance and early warning systems.

THE JET AGE BEGINS

The power and promise of jet propulsion technology was validated in the later stages of World War II. New German jet fighters, with their blazing speed and acceleration, showed signs of dominating the skies over Europe but were not produced in sufficient quantities to shift the war's momentum. Nevertheless, the U.S. War Department had to quickly level the playing field.

On June 8, 1943, General Hap Arnold approved a contract for Lockheed to counter the German threat. Over the next six months, Johnson's team toiled 10 hours a day, six days a week in their improvised tent facility, which sat downwind of a plastics factory that produced noxious odors. As legend has it, an engineer once jokingly entered the tent wearing a gas mask to fend off the fumes. The name "Skunk Works" was soon adopted for the covert facility, inspired by the popular comic strip "Li'l Abner," in which the "Skonk Works" factory produced a foul-smelling oil made of skunks and old shoes.

White Sands Proving Ground, New Mexico.

M-3118

Kelly Johnson shakes hands with test pilot Milo Burcham after the first flight of XP-80. On January 8, 1944, Burcham climbed into the cockpit of the jet aircraft. "Find out if she's a lady or a witch,"[4] Johnson instructed. The plane handled beautifully and the prototype earned the ladylike name *Lulu Belle*.

Despite the stench, Lockheed's Skunk Works team delivered the sleek XP-80 jet fighter prototype in 143 days, 37 days ahead of schedule. The forthcoming production line was dubbed the "Shooting Star" in honor of its unparalleled speed and in keeping with the Lockheed tradition of naming aircraft after celestial bodies. Later models were capable of coming close to 600 mph in level flight.

The P-80 was kept out of battle in World War II so as not to allow that technology to fall into enemy hands. Still, the fighter plane would soon find its way to the front lines.

MARTIN'S GAMBLE

In the postwar years, Martin made its own gamble on the commercial airline industry. Rather than compete with the larger Lockheed Constellation or its chief rival, the Douglas DC-6, Martin aimed to fill a market gap by producing a medium-range aircraft. The effort yielded the twin-engine piston Martin 2-0-2, with seating for 44, and later the 4-0-4, a pressurized version of the same aircraft. Early sales were promising, with 17 companies in the United States, Chile and Venezuela ordering more than 300 of the airliners.

As was the case with the Lockheed Constellation, Howard Hughes became the Martin aircraft's key customer, buying 12 of the 2-0-2s and 41 of the 4-0-4s for TWA to complement his fleet of longer-range Connies.

Meanwhile, heritage company Convair (formed from the 1943 merger of the Consolidated and Vultee aircraft companies) soon followed Martin's lead and produced its own mid-sized airliners. An unfortunate series of production delays, structural mishaps, contractual loopholes and Glenn Martin's basic generosity allowed companies to cancel their orders without penalty. The Convair 240 stole the lion's share of the market, and by the end of 1947, Martin recorded a net loss of $19 million. The die was cast. The commercial market soon proved less fruitful than Martin had hoped.

Fortunately, Martin placed bets elsewhere, developing "pilotless systems" that would forever change the aircraft industry.

The third of four Martin 2-0-2s purchased by Chilean airline Linea Aerea Nacional (LAN) in flight over the U.S. Naval Academy in Annapolis, Md., 1949.

COMMERCIAL AVIATION: FLIGHT OF THE CONNIES

While not a Skunk Works project per se, one of the most revered and graceful aircraft created during World War II was also a clandestine development.

Back in 1939, the top brass of the Lockheed Corporation — president Robert Gross, chief engineer Hall Hibbard and Kelly Johnson — had scheduled a key meeting with a man with deep pockets who had set aviation records in Lockheed planes: Howard Hughes.

Hughes hoped to hire Lockheed to design a revolutionary aircraft capable of comfortably shuttling 20 passengers and 6,000 pounds of cargo across the United States in commercial aviation's first coast-to-coast, nonstop service. Lockheed had endeavored to build an aircraft that "would carry more people farther and faster than ever before, and economically enough to broaden the acceptance of flying as an alternative to train, ship and automobile,"[5] Johnson said. Hughes persuaded the team to think bigger than the original design for the Model 44 Excalibur. As a result, the Constellation was born.

Hughes, a majority stakeholder in TWA, saw the new plane — called Connie for short — as his secret weapon in the commercial air travel industry. He treated the project with all the subterfuge that secret weapons require: Not only did he demand total secrecy, he also specified that Lockheed could not sell the aircraft to any other transcontinental airline until TWA had received 35 of them.

The Constellation offered the first hydraulically boosted power controls, aviation's equivalent of power steering. It was faster than most World War II fighters at 350 mph. And using award-winning technology pioneered by Lockheed a few years earlier, it featured a pressurized cabin for 44 passengers that allowed the plane to fly faster and above 90 percent of weather disturbances — what Constellation regulars would come to call "smooth sailing."

Howard Hughes brought fame to the Constellation through traditional advertising — and by breaking a transcontinental speed record on a flight from Burbank to Washington, D.C., in April 1944 with Jack Frye of TWA. Ever the showman, Hughes stopped during his return flight in Dayton, Ohio, to pick up aviation pioneer Orville Wright (pictured at right), who made his last flight as copilot of the Connie.

In fact, Lockheed's design was so good that the U.S. military saw its potential as a transport for troops and supplies in Europe. The military assumed control of production in 1942. The first official flight test for a Constellation, sheathed in olive green paint and redesignated the C-69, came early the next year. When the war ended, TWA bought back all the C-69s it could from the government; conversions were made, and the Constellation entered commercial service in February 1946.

While only 13 Constellations were built during World War II — Lockheed was asked to focus instead on the P-38 — the Army, Air Force and Navy had recognized the plane's versatility. By 1948, the Navy was calling in orders for Connies to act as long-range patrol aircraft, nicknamed Po-Boys from the PO-1 designation then in use. In time, Constellations would be used for everything from rescue missions and VIP transports to airborne early warning missions and the mapping of Earth's magnetic field to serving as the support aircraft for both the Navy's Blue Angels and Air Force's Thunderbirds.

Orville Wright, who achieved the world's first manned, powered, sustained and controlled flight in an airplane, made his last flight as copilot of the C-69 Connie at Wright Field in Dayton, Ohio, in 1944.

The Martin Matador offered significant breakthroughs in propulsion, guidance and launch procedure. It was propelled by a turbo jet for cruising in flight and a solid rocket booster that ejected from the aircraft's body after launch.

"THE ACHIEVEMENT OF A SATELLITE CRAFT BY THE UNITED STATES WOULD INFLAME THE IMAGINATION OF MANKIND."[6]

—RAND CORPORATION, 1946

BEYOND GRAVITY

Both Lockheed and Martin attempted to make inroads in commercial aviation while seeking postwar military and government contracts. While Lockheed's efforts during and immediately after World War II focused on propeller- and jet-powered aircraft, Martin set its sights beyond the stratosphere, employing the deceptively simple yet powerful principles of rocket propulsion.

The nascent field of rocket technology became the basis for both long-range ballistic missiles and space exploration. Both would play a key role in the coming Cold War, as the United States and the Soviet Union each raced to develop a technological edge.

VIKING AND MATADOR

While the United States and the Soviet Union developed nuclear deterrents behind the scenes, conquering space soon became humanity's great challenge. The notion of reaching beyond the bounds of Earth was an ideological proxy for the supremacy of the two superpowers, but the scientific and even spiritual value of accomplishing spaceflight offered its own rewards.

Gaining greater understanding of the upper atmosphere was the next steppingstone. Working with the Naval Research Laboratory, Martin won the contract in 1946 to develop and build the Viking series of sounding rockets. Twelve Viking rockets were ultimately launched from White Sands Proving Ground, each with different features and scientific objectives. Numerous trials ensued, with Vikings setting altitude records repeatedly. By 1954, Viking 11 rose to a record altitude of 158 miles and took the first photographs of Earth from space. The Viking series thus built a foundation of upper atmospheric knowledge, helping measure temperature, pressure, wind shear, electron density and ultraviolet spectra. These insights encouraged rocket engineers to push the technology higher, developing multistage rockets with more powerful engines potentially capable of launching a man-made artifact into orbit. The Viking's potential as a ballistic missile was also explored, but Martin already led the way in this field, creating the country's first operational surface-to-surface tactical missile: the TM-61 Matador.

A TM-76A Mace missile, successor to the TM-61 Matador, launching from a dual-missile shelter, 1960.

The Martin TM-61 Matador, a winged, pilotless aircraft, was first launched from White Sands Proving Ground in 1949. A new radio guidance system allowed for midflight course corrections. Matador's portability gave it flexible deployment options and the ability to launch "using a geographic footprint only as large as the missile itself … a revolutionary launch system developed for the Matador called 'Zero Length Launch.'"[7] All told, Martin produced 971 Matador missiles between 1949 and 1957. Another 295 of the longer-range and improved-guidance TM-76 Mace missiles were later produced.

As Martin's focus widened to include missiles and rockets, the company undertook a handful of airplane projects for the Navy and Air Force from the late 1940s until the late 1950s. Hans Multhopp designed an experimental tactical jet bomber, the XB-51. It featured a swept-wing design — a shift that soon proved necessary for high-speed

The Viking 4 was tested in a launch from the deck of USS *Norton Sound*, 1950.

and supersonic jet aircraft whose straight-wing designs suffered shockwaves when approaching the sound barrier. Another Martin innovation on the XB-51 was its rotating bomb bay door, which promoted greater efficiency in ordnance loading.

Despite these innovations, the Air Force did not develop the XB-51. The Air Force instead asked Martin to produce a modified version of a British bomber, soon designated the Martin B-57 Canberra. More than 400 of the B-57s were produced in various configurations, with some modified by Convair for reconnaissance flights above 60,000 feet. During this period, Martin also continued to produce sea planes for the Navy. Two models, the P5M Marlin, which would be the U.S. Navy's last operational flying boat, and the jet-powered P6M SeaMaster, a developmental sea plane that didn't go into production immediately, put a punctuation mark on Glenn L. Martin's four decades at the helm of the company, effectively coming full circle on a storied legacy of sea plane design and manufacturing that began with the Martin Model 12's record-setting flight in May 1912.

NUCLEAR PAYLOADS

Martin's shift from planes to missiles dovetailed with the dawn of the nuclear age. The ability to deliver atomic payloads to targets thousands of miles away became a core facet of the military's deterrent strategy. While Martin's early work on rockets and missiles served this purpose in part, Lockheed and Convair stuck with their core competency, producing two important high-payload, long-range and nuclear-capable aircraft.

THE ABILITY TO DELIVER ATOMIC PAYLOADS TO TARGETS THOUSANDS OF MILES AWAY BECAME A CORE FACET OF THE MILITARY'S DETERRENT STRATEGY.

First flown in May 1945, the crew of this P2V Neptune (nicknamed the *Truculent Turtle*) set a new long-distance world record in 1946, flying 11,236 miles nonstop from Perth, Australia, to Port Columbus, Ohio, without aerial refueling. The record stands today. The Neptune was the first land plane designed specifically for the Navy's antisubmarine warfare mission.

The largest American warplane ever created, the Convair B-36, could fly 4,000 miles with an 80,000-pound payload. The first B-36 was introduced in August 1946. Just three year later, some B-36 models could reach top speeds of 435 mph, a 50,000-foot ceiling, and a range of up to 12,000 miles, solidifying their position as an intimidating long-distance bomber and vital reconnaissance aircraft.

By 1947, the U.S. Navy and the Air Force were both seeking new technologies that could effectively deliver nuclear munitions overseas. As a proof point for the Navy, a Lockheed P2V-3C Neptune flew on April 7, 1949, from the USS *Midway* (CV-41) off the Virginia Capes on a 4,000-mile mission to California — carrying a 74,000-pound payload and dropping a dummy bomb the size and weight of a nuclear weapon — before returning to the Naval Air Test Center at Naval Air Station Patuxent River in Maryland. The Air Force had its own dog in the hunt: the Convair B-36. Sitting on the runway, the B-36 turned heads. The 163-foot-long behemoth, with its 230-foot wingspan and six rear-facing four-row radial engines, dwarfed every other warplane in America's arsenal. As one pilot later remarked, flying a B-36 was "like sitting in a bay window flying an apartment house."[8]

On December 7, 1948, Lt. Col. John Bartlett flew from Carswell Air Force Base in Texas to Hawaii, dropped a dummy bomb on an assigned target and headed back home. When Bartlett returned, having successfully hit his target without needing to refuel, U.S. military officials realized the B-36's potential. If Bartlett could fly from Texas to Hawaii and return home, he could fly round-trip from Maine to Leningrad, counterbalancing the threats of missile attacks from bellicose Russian generals in the East. In the B-36, the United States had found a powerful deterrent against Soviet aggression and selected the Air Force's bomber for procurement.

Unfortunately, the rapid advance of technology would catch up with the B-36. An updated YB-60 prototype with redesigned swept wings and eight jet engines elevated the plane's speed to 508 mph, but a new generation of swifter high-payload bombers was already on the horizon. Officially, the B-36 never saw combat action and never dropped a bomb on an enemy target, but it was the only plane of its era capable of delivering nuclear payloads to intercontinental targets, and the *Peacemaker* thus remained a powerful deterrent until it was officially retired in 1959.

U.S. Gen. Douglas MacArthur watches the advance of ground troops while flying over Korea's Yalu River in his Lockheed C-121 Constellation, nicknamed *Bataan*, on Nov. 26, 1950.

THE COLD WAR BEGINS

Despite the B-36's moniker, peace was elusive in the postwar era. In April 1948, the Soviets blockaded supply lines into West Berlin to consolidate control of the former German capital. A U.S.-led task force soon began airlifting supplies to the 2 million citizens and Allied troops in Berlin, ultimately delivering 2.3 million tons of vital necessities through September 1949, several months after the Soviets pulled their blockade in May 1949.

To address the continued instability in Europe and Asia, the United Nations officially formed in October 1945. From 1946 to 1952, the U.N. was headquartered at Lockheed Martin heritage company Sperry Gyroscope Corporation in Lake Success, N.Y., chosen for its large, modern and air-conditioned spaces that could host delegations in a centralized location. Next, in the wake of the Berlin blockade, the North Atlantic Treaty Organization formed in April 1949 as a unified military defense organization. Fears were stoked with the Soviet detonation of its first atomic bomb on Aug. 29, 1949. Communist regimes established in late 1949 by China's Mao Zedong and in early 1950 by North Vietnam's Ho Chi Minh further motivated NATO countries to curtail the spread of communism.

The F-94C Starfire variant was reconfigured to accommodate many updated features, including nose-mounted rockets, an automatic pilot system, closed-breech launchers and drag chute for reduced airframe stress during landing, 1953.

P-80 Shooting Stars flying in formation, 1951.

The slow simmer finally boiled over on June 25, 1950, when the Soviet-supported communist government of North Korea crossed the 38th parallel dividing line and invaded U.S.-backed South Korea, setting off a prolonged and inconclusive war of attrition.

THE KOREAN WAR

The Korean War involved less air warfare than either side expected, and ultimately hearkened back to World War I's ground and trench warfare. Still, NATO air forces supported ground attacks and held the early advantage in air superiority, with Lockheed's newly redesignated F-80 Shooting Stars (F stood for fighter; the World War II aircrafts used P for pursuit) playing a leading role. Some 75 percent of enemy losses during the initial months of the Korean campaign were attributed to air attacks by Shooting Stars. The opposition could do little to match the Lockheed jet fighter.

THE MISSILE WITH A MAN IN IT

In 1952, Kelly Johnson traveled to Korea, touring some 23,000 miles in an Air Force Connie and visiting 15 air bases to gain firsthand knowledge of battlefront conditions. He wanted to learn what pilots needed from Lockheed. "It was unanimous," Johnson later wrote. "They wanted speed and altitude." Johnson began designing what would become the F-104 Starfighter, later known as the "Missile With a Man in It."[9]

Though it did not fly until after the Korean War, a plane like the F-104 Starfighter was desperately needed by West Germany, now a critical new member of NATO and a defensive buffer between its allies in the West and the Soviets in the East. An inexpensive lightweight fighter with thin and short 7-foot wings, sharp as daggers, the F-104 was quickly recognized as the most elite air combat aircraft of its day. It was capable of reaching Mach 2, and later versions were sturdy enough to weather any storm. It was the perfect NATO warplane.

Lockheed sent experts to teach West German engineers how to properly translate Lockheed plans, technical orders and unfamiliar parts into actual fighters. Lockheed then ensured sound production cycles by developing the Starfighter Utilization Reliability Effort, which sent aerodynamicists, pilots and service reps to troubleshoot issues as they arose.

The collaboration between the West German government and Lockheed was so successful, in fact, that other nations quickly followed suit, purchasing licensing rights for the aircraft over the ensuing decades.

An R-2 rocket fitted above the jet engine boosts the NF-104 Starfighter into the upper atmosphere for high-altitude astronaut training at Edwards Air Force Base, 1957.

A pilot ejects via a rocket-propelled cockpit seat from an F-104 rocket test sled at Edwards Air Force Base, 1950s. Ejection seats greatly reduced the number of pilot casualties.

After the secrecy of the aircraft's early development phase, the F-104 Starfighter makes its press debut at Palmdale Air Force Base, 1956.

That remained true only until October 1950, when China intervened to assist its North Korean allies, deploying the Soviet-designed MiG-15 fighter jet. Its swept-wing design, powerful engine and simple construction made the new aircraft dangerous in combat and efficient to mass-produce. While the F-80 won the first jet-versus-jet dogfight against the MiG, the Soviet jet was ultimately faster and soon outclassed and outnumbered the F-80, creating demand for a faster and higher-altitude NATO fighter plane. Subsequent iterations of the P-80, like the P-80B (which introduced the first ejection seat in a production U.S. aircraft), the speedy T-33 trainer (which remained in service until 1997) and the F-94 (the world's first all-weather interceptor) helped fill this need.

Aside from replacing the F-80 as a more advanced and versatile fighter plane against the MiG-15, the F-94 was designed to intercept the growing numbers of Soviet Tupolev Tu-4 bombers being produced. When the Korean War ended in a stalemate on July 27, 1953, little about the regional influences had changed from their prewar state. However, in the intervening years, Soviet manufacturers had ramped up production of their own long-range bombers. By the mid-1950s, the Soviets seemed capable of matching the Convair B-36 with their own viable intercontinental bomber that could deliver nuclear payloads from Russia to the United States.

FROM MARTIN TO BUNKER
In the early 1950s, Martin was still underwater as a result of its underachieving commercial airliner projects but was kept from bankruptcy because of its production efforts supporting the Korean War. Employment at Martin had grown from a modest 7,400 in 1949 to 22,000 in 1952, but Martin's plane-making future — indeed, the solvency of the company itself — was very much in jeopardy. It was time for founder Glenn L. Martin to step aside and open the door for a new generation of leadership.

MIT graduate and former Trailmobile Corporation Chairman George Maverick Bunker arrived in Baltimore on Feb. 21, 1952, ready to take the reins of a 40-year-old company deep in debt. At the ensuing board meeting, Bunker — who had previously manufactured truck trailers — was elected president and chief executive, and Martin was made honorary board chairman. The following year, Martin was selected for the

SOME 75 PERCENT OF ENEMY LOSSES DURING THE INITIAL MONTHS OF THE KOREAN CAMPAIGN WERE ATTRIBUTED TO AIR ATTACKS BY SHOOTING STARS.
THE OPPOSITION COULD DO LITTLE TO MATCH THE LOCKHEED JET FIGHTER.

second time to deliver the prestigious Wright Brothers Lecture to the Institute of Aeronautical Sciences, marking the 50th anniversary of powered flight. Martin, in turn, honored the many hands that built the aircraft industry:

> The modern airplane constitutes an integration of thoughts and lifetime work of more individuals than any other industry on earth. ... This interplay of really diverse avenues of human effort is a monument to man's dependence upon other men.[10]

Similarly, George Maverick Bunker envisioned Martin as a company destined for diversification, producing everything from rockets and missiles to electronics and communications devices. What Bunker needed, however, was a name to encapsulate it all, so he coined one. He called them aerospace technologies, and he bet the company's future on them.

REVOLUTION IN RECON

On May 1, 1954, leaders across the Washington, D.C., intelligence community found themselves breaking out in a cold sweat. Over the skies of Red Square in Moscow, the Soviet Union had just introduced its newest bomber — the Myasishchev M-4, ominously nicknamed *Hammer* — during a Russian May Day celebration.

Glenn L. Martin (left) and his successor, George Maverick Bunker, 1952

Coming on the heels of the Soviet Union's successful detonation of a hydrogen bomb the previous summer, the unveiling fueled a growing fear that Russia had not only eclipsed the West in terms of nuclear weapons and bomber production but could also be gearing up for a potential attack on the United States. The country needed a long-range aircraft that could fly at extremely high altitudes above enemy interceptors and return home with vital Soviet reconnaissance data.

In the summer of 1954, Kelly Johnson went to Washington under strict secrecy to share his ideas for a lightweight high-altitude reconnaissance aircraft capable of flying above the reach of Soviet anti-aircraft fire. For three days, a team of scientists and engineers picked apart his proposed design for the so-called U-2, which borrowed its sleek looks from the profile of a traditional sailplane.

President Eisenhower and CIA Director Allen Dulles had already signed off on two competing designs for a high-altitude reconnaissance aircraft, but Johnson was undeterred. He knew he had the better design. So he offered to assume complete responsibility for the aircraft's future maintenance and service — an entirely new concept in aviation — and promised a nearly impossible turnaround time for having the plane in the air.

Johnson's track record spoke for itself, and he returned to Burbank's Skunk Works with a green light to gather a covert crew and begin work on a reconnaissance plane initially dubbed *The Angel from Paradise Ranch* and later known worldwide as the iconic U-2, which would later pick up its nickname, Dragon Lady, from the Milton Caniff cartoon "Terry and The Pirates." Under CIA direction and funding, Johnson and about 80 members of the Skunk Works team worked like mad. The spirit of the division was captured perfectly on July 15, 1955, in an entry from Johnson's logbook: "Airplane essentially completed. Terrifically long hours. Everybody almost dead."[11]

The long, tapered wing of the U-2, shown here in 1955, allowed it to fly 3,000-mile missions and carry up to 700 pounds of photoreconnaissance equipment to a staggering and unprecedented altitude of 70,000 feet.

Incredibly, Johnson delivered the first U-2 for a test flight on July 29, 1955, only nine months after signing the contract. The plane was disassembled and brought to Nevada, where famed test pilot Tony LeVier first flew the U-2 on August 4, 1955. Johnson recalled the excitement after the plane's first flight:

Under the direction of the CIA, a Skunk Works team of about 80 worked grueling hours to deliver a U-2 for test flight on July 29, 1955, in Nevada.

That night all of us celebrated with the usual beer and arm-wrestling contests. Thanks to my early lathing work, I was pretty good at both. It has been our policy in the Skunk Works that everyone — all the workers as well as the engineers and executives — sees the first flight and is included in the traditional party afterward.[12]

The U-2 was then flown four days later for the Washington brass. President Eisenhower had his secret weapon, and he was determined to use it to prevent the Cold War from overheating.

SETTING OFF THE SPACE RACE

Soon, President Eisenhower came to a similar conclusion as Bunker and placed a major bet on aerospace. On July 29, 1955, he announced that the United States would place an artificial satellite in Earth's orbit within 18 months. The announcement effectively kicked off the space race.

America's hopes to place a satellite in orbit were put on the Martin-led Project Vanguard. The Vanguard family of rockets evolved from the Viking series, this time incorporating a three-stage launch vehicle, and Martin was awarded the Vanguard contract on October 7, 1955. Adding to a string of successes, Martin next beat competitors Lockheed and Douglas for an equally high-profile Air Force contract to build the LGM-25 Titan I ICBM, awarded only months after the Vanguard project.

In early 1956, Bunker flew to Huntsville, Ala., for what he anticipated would be a routine courtesy call to an Army major general named John Bruce. Bunker and his company were on a roll. He had recently authorized the construction of a new facility in Denver to work on the Titan missile program, while other Martin teams plugged away at the Vanguard system for the Navy. Profits were up. Work was steady. The course was set. But when Bunker sat down for his meeting, he was surprised to hear Bruce offer an unusual confession.

What the Army could really use, Bruce said, was a company to come along and build a plant between Huntsville and Cape Canaveral, Fla., the primary launch site for long-range missiles.

Bunker said his goodbyes and flew home. By the fall, he had quietly authorized the purchase of 6,777 acres near a then-sleepy central Florida town called Orlando. It was a huge risk — building such a massive plant without a secured project to keep it busy. But Bunker believed his company's growing leadership in missiles, rockets and aerospace would soon compel the Army as it had the Air Force and Navy. This was a risk Martin needed to take.

While Martin continued to lead the way in missile and rocket manufacturing, Soviet Premier Nikita Khrushchev declared in 1956 that his country was making "missiles like sausages" and that he would soon have a hydrogen bomb capable of striking "any point in the world."[13] Any uninvited guests flying over Russia, he also warned, would be shot down. American concerns about a "bomber gap" grew increasingly dire, with many believing the Soviets had gained a serious advantage. It was up to Lockheed's U-2 to learn the truth.

On July 4, 1956, Hervey Stockman flew a U-2 from West Germany deep into the heart of the Soviet Union, capturing detailed photos of airfields, factories and shipyards previously unattainable by other aircraft. The plane was tracked by Soviet radar, but Stockman's U-2 flew beyond the reach of Soviet interceptors and anti-aircraft fire, returning home with history-altering intelligence.

U-2 overflights revealed that the Soviets were more concerned with building tractors than tanks. Russia's ability to produce high-end bombers was unimpressive at best. Its missiles, while numerous, were better suited for intermediate attacks against Europe than long-range attacks on the United States, with most unprepared to fire at all. Thanks to the U-2, Eisenhower had the information he needed to avert a massive arms buildup — and a potential war.

Khrushchev's braggadocio, however, contained kernels of truth. After the Soviets unexpectedly invaded Hungary in November 1956, Eisenhower redeployed the U-2 on reconnaissance flights, and in August 1957, a U-2 confirmed the existence of a potential ICBM launch site at Tyuratam, Kazakhstan. Several weeks later, the Soviets had indeed successfully tested the RS-7, the world's first operational ICBM. Fearing

Propaganda posters from the 1950s like this one celebrated the Soviet Union's fleeting advantage in the space race.

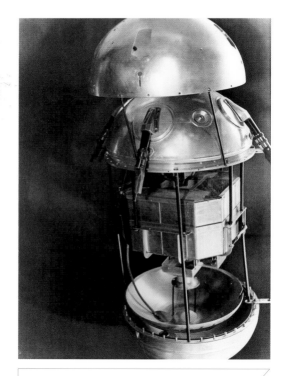

Only 23 inches in diameter, Sputnik 1 contained two radio transmitters, a series of batteries and a thermometer, as shown in this exploded view of the mocked-up sphere.

the worst — an intercontinental nuclear attack — the U.S. Air Force's Strategic Air Command soon initiated an around-the-clock alert, which remained in effect until 1991. The country braced for nuclear war.

The Soviets launched another rocket on October 4, 1957. But instead of carrying a nuclear warhead toward Europe or North America, the booster successfully lifted the world's first man-made satellite into space. The small, simple and symbolic aluminum sphere — Sputnik, Russian for "traveler" — orbited the planet at 18,000 mph. As Sputnik's telltale radio signal transmitted its beeps back to Earth, the underlying message was clear: The Soviets had beaten the Americans into space. But the race was far from over.

On Aug. 5, 1957, a Lockheed U-2 found and photographed the Soviet missile test site at Tyuratam, known as the Baikonur Cosmodrome. This was the launch pad for the R-7 missile that sent Sputnik into orbit.

CHAPTER 5

LAUNCH PADS

The Space Race

1957–1969

"WE WERE IN A PIONEERING STAGE, BECAUSE NOBODY HAD GONE INTO SPACE BEFORE. ... WE HAD TO INVENT SCIENCE... AND THE LAUNCH PAD WAS ACTUALLY OUR FACTORY."[1]

—MINORU "SAM" ARAKI

PUBLIC FAILURES, SECRET TRIUMPHS

It was December 6, 1957, and news cameras were rolling. At T-minus 60 minutes, the gantry crane pulled away from the Martin Vanguard TV-3, set to be the first U.S. launch attempt since the Soviets launched Sputnik. At T-minus 45 seconds, the umbilical cords supplying air and electricity were disconnected, leaving the rocket standing alone on its Cape Canaveral launch pad.

A gantry crane lifts into position the first stage of the Martin Vanguard satellite launch vehicle, 1957. [INSET] The Agena was the satellite platform for Project Discoverer/Corona and six American satellites.

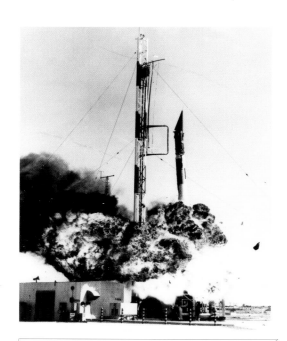

The 1957 explosion of the Martin Vanguard TV-3 led to a new testing procedure that soon spread to other organizations within Martin. Soon, a far-reaching and influential program developed that affected not only America's space program but also nearly every quality control program in the world: Zero Defects.

At T-minus 1 second, a Martin engineer flipped a switch in the blockhouse control room, and an anxious team waited for ignition. The world held its breath. The Vanguard engine roared to life, and the rocket lifted into the air. And then, after rising only 4 feet off its platform, it slammed back down into its cradle, detonating a powerful explosion of fuel and fire.

America had already lost the race to put the first satellite in space, and now the botched Vanguard launch — quickly dubbed "Kaputnik" or "Flopnik" by newspapers worldwide — was immediately burned into the nation's psyche. After its very public failure, Project Vanguard redeemed itself, ultimately placing four satellites in orbit, beginning with TV-4 in December 1958. But as TV-3 had proved, launching rockets was no easy task and left no room for error. Given this fine line between triumph and disaster and the deepening distrust between Soviets and Americans, the decision to either publicize or conceal space projects became another delicate dance.

Lockheed's Corona project, publicly known as Project Discoverer, was one of the top-secret ones. With national security at stake, President Eisenhower made access to reliable intelligence about the USSR a top priority. The United States needed to know everything it could about Soviet military strength, nuclear capabilities and mobilization.

The U-2's role in collecting photoreconnaissance over the Soviet Union is well known. But while Kelly Johnson's Skunk Works team was racing to develop the iconic Dragon Lady, another small team of innovative Lockheed engineers in California was hard at work on another high-flying intelligence asset: the world's first photoreconnaissance satellite.

Imagine the challenge of taking pictures from space without a digital camera or a high-speed wireless communications link to the ground. Corona took photos the old-fashioned way — on 70 mm film, specially designed by Eastman Kodak for space operations. Each satellite carried two enormous canisters of film — initially about 5,000 linear feet (it was later expanded even further). Each individual photo covered 1,200 square miles of land.

On August 19, 1960, the Discoverer/Corona 14 dropped its film from space. Once it entered the Earth's atmosphere, a parachute deployed and the recovery capsule was caught midair at an altitude of 8,000 feet.

When the film was spent, Corona tucked each canister into a hardened "bucket" and dropped it from space back to Earth. When the bucket entered the atmosphere, usually over the Pacific Ocean, it would deploy a parachute, and an Air Force plane fitted with a unique hook and net device would fly by and catch it in midair. Corona became much more than a delicate dance. It was some of the most complex covert choreography ever attempted.

These simultaneous public and private space races characterized aerospace work in the 1960s. Corona and other vital reconnaissance projects kept the Cold War from boiling over. Meanwhile, as competition between the United States and the Soviet Union grew increasingly fierce, a spectacular series of trials and errors in the burgeoning fields of missiles and space systems pressed humanity ever closer to a shared goal: traveling beyond Earth.

Though initially designed to carry nuclear warheads, an Atlas-B rocket successfully launched the Signal Communications by Orbiting Relay Equipment, the United States' first communications satellite, on Dec. 18, 1958, and delivered Eisenhower's Christmas greeting to the world.

SOVIET SUCCESSES, AMERICAN RESPONSES

In the late 1950s, a human being who could enter space, orbit Earth and return safely was still the brass ring of the international space race. Just as early aviators had struggled to make rapid travel across vast oceans and land masses a reality, the idea of humans completing a round-trip flight to the moon — or beyond — was seen by many as a pipe dream. To achieve the impossible, both the United States and the Soviet Union had to develop, refine, integrate and test numerous systems:

- Launch vehicles to carry payloads into space
- Manned spacecraft to carry humans atop these rockets
- Life support and pilot training systems to keep human space travelers alive and well
- Remote command centers to control the spacecraft in orbit
- Re-entry plans to safely bring spacecraft and astronauts back to Earth.

As the Americans played catch-up, the Soviets logged a string of early victories. After Sputnik 1 in October 1957, the Soviets followed up a month later with the R-7, which launched the first living being into orbit — a dog named Laika. Their Luna 2 satellite next made a planned crash-landing on the moon in 1959, and Luna 3 captured photos of its far side, never before seen by anyone on Earth.

However, the U.S. program remained determined to succeed. In July 1958, President Dwight D. Eisenhower signed the National Aeronautics and Space Act, creating the National Aeronautics and Space Administration, formerly the National Advisory Committee for Aeronautics, established in 1915. An initial series of satellite launches propelled the U.S. program closer to the ultimate aim of the race — manned spaceflight — and the Convair Atlas, Lockheed Agena, and later, Martin Titan rockets made up the core of NASA's launch vehicles.

Thin-skinned but incredibly powerful, the Convair Atlas family of rockets was born in 1957 as the first successful intercontinental ballistic missile launched by the United States. Atlas' lightweight stainless-steel skin kept its shape partly because of the highly pressurized fuel it carried. The era's most venerable rocket designer, Wernher von Braun, felt the Atlas would not survive the stresses of launch, calling it no more than a blimp. But the Atlas would repeatedly prove von Braun wrong.

The Atlas legacy includes more than 100 scientific missions completed from 1960 to 1978, including Mariner 4's flyby of Mars in 1964, which delivered the first up-close photographs of the Red Planet. Though Atlas began as an ICBM to deter the Soviet Union, today's Atlas V is built with a Russian-designed RD-180 rocket engine.

... THE CONVAIR ATLAS FAMILY OF ROCKETS WAS BORN IN 1957 AS THE FIRST SUCCESSFUL INTERCONTINENTAL BALLISTIC MISSILE LAUNCHED BY THE UNITED STATES.

Relying on Atlas as well as Redstone launch vehicles, the U.S. effort to send a human into space officially began October 7, 1958, with the green light for NASA's Project Mercury. Going head to head with the Soviets, the United States gathered a team of military test pilots who soon began an intensive training regimen designed to prepare them for the physical and psychological challenges of space.

These pioneering astronauts would be forever known as the Mercury Seven.

Pilot Francis Gary Powers with the Lockheed U-2 Dragon Lady high-altitude reconnaissance aircraft, 1955.

SECRECY AND PUBLICITY

Though the Soviet Union initially referred to their would-be space explorers as astronauts, they changed their term to cosmonauts to differentiate their space program from America's. The differences between the Soviet and U.S. programs, however, extended far beyond nomenclature.

America's Mercury Seven astronauts were immediately thrust into the public eye. An exclusive deal with LIFE magazine in August 1959 paid them $500,000 for exclusive access to their professional efforts, as well as their personal lives. Conversely, Russian cosmonauts earned about $100 a month. The details of the Soviet program remained hushed, as did the identities of its cosmonauts. Soviet test launches, especially failed attempts, were cloaked in secrecy.

This contrast between Soviet secrecy and American publicity was soon turned upside down. On May 1, 1960, Korean War veteran Francis Gary Powers, piloting a Lockheed U-2C Dragon Lady high-altitude reconnaissance aircraft, was sent on an extended overflight of the Soviet Union as part of Operation Grand Slam. Hoping to gain vital intelligence on ICBMs and spacecraft capabilities at the Tyuratam launch site, as well as other far-flung sites such as Sverdlovsk and Plesetsk, Powers aimed to survey more of the Soviet Union than any previous U-2 mission had covered.

But four hours after taking off from a military airbase in Pakistan, Powers was shot down over Sverdlovsk by a Soviet surface-to-air missile. The U-2 fell from 70,000 feet to 30,000 feet. Powers was able to eject from the cockpit but could not trigger the self-destruct mechanism that might have protected the secrets of the U-2 aircraft or its photographic findings. He was subsequently captured, imprisoned and interrogated by the KGB. Soviet Premier Nikita Khrushchev turned the tables on the United States. Powers was placed on public trial and eventually sentenced to 10 years in prison and hard labor, while pieces of the downed U-2 plane were exhibited in Moscow.

The incident came at an inauspicious time. A planned Paris Summit scheduled for May 14 could have been an opportunity to reduce tensions between the Cold War opponents, but on the heels of the U-2 conflict, Khrushchev demanded a public apology from Eisenhower for violating Soviet airspace. When Eisenhower refused, Khrushchev abandoned the summit. Eisenhower was forced to cancel future U-2 overflights, leaving a dangerous gap in U.S. reconnaissance. To fill that gap, Eisenhower authorized one of the most ambitious space projects to date. It began with a bang.

Soviet leader Nikita Khrushchev displayed the wreckage of Francis Gary Powers' U-2 in Gorky Park, 1960.

Powers was ultimately released from KGB custody and returned to the United States in exchange for Soviet superspy Rudolf Abel in February 1962. Powers holds a model of the U-2 as he begins testimony before the Senate Armed Services Committee, 1962.

MAPPING THE CLOUDS

During the Francis Gary Powers U-2 incident, Eisenhower and U.S. military leaders first claimed the aircraft was an unarmed weather research plane that had strayed off course and accidentally violated Soviet airspace. But by this time, weather research and observation itself was moving to even higher ground.

Lockheed Martin heritage company Radio Corporation of America successfully launched the world's first weather satellite on April 1, 1960. The Television and InfraRed

Observation Satellite (TIROS-I) demonstrated the advantage of mapping Earth's cloud cover from satellite altitudes. The first views revealed clouds banded and clustered in unexpected ways. The mission also succeeded in verifying experimental television techniques designed to develop a worldwide meteorological satellite information system, and testing sun angle and horizon sensor systems for spacecraft orientation. This premier weather satellite built on decades of television technology pioneered by RCA.

The Television InfraRed Observation Satellite (TIROS) was produced for the National Oceanographic and Atmospheric Administration and NASA in 1960.

A SPY IN THE SKY

On May 17, 1956, an explosion rocked Sunnyvale, Calif. Lockheed President Courtlandt Gross had organized the purchase of about 400 acres of land close to the intellectual mecca of Palo Alto's Stanford Industrial Park. Rather than shoveling dirt or cutting a ceremonial ribbon, the company chose to break ground by detonating a charge of powder. The resulting blast symbolically prepared for the rocket-fueled future of a new initiative that would soon call Sunnyvale home: Lockheed Missiles & Space Division.

Formed in November 1955, LMSD carved out a prominent place for itself on the defense contracting map because of two major projects: the U.S. Navy's Fleet Ballistic Missile program and the USAF's advanced military satellite systems contract authorized by Eisenhower and known initially as WS-117L. The mandate soon morphed into three subsystems known as Discoverer, SAMOS and MIDAS, created to fulfill the post-World War II need for photoreconnaissance and early-warning missile defense. These national priorities became increasingly urgent after the launch of Sputnik.

All three systems initially relied on the Lockheed-developed Agena upper-stage vehicle. Featuring a three-axis stabilization system, the Agena provided an unprecedented level of orbital control. When mated with launch vehicles like the Thor, Atlas or Titan boosters, the Agena scored numerous "firsts" in the space race and soon became the workhorse satellite of the 1960s and '70s.[2] Some of the Agena's earliest and greatest tests came in service of the far-reaching Discoverer/Corona.

TRIAL AND ERROR

In 1958, Eisenhower gave the Air Force and the CIA just nine months to put Corona, the first recon satellite, on the launch pad — a nearly impossible task. Racing against the clock, a team of the brightest minds from government and industry started with just a one-page specification document, rolled up their sleeves and got to work.

"We were directed to launch in nine months, even though we had no knowledge of the environment or physics of space, no satellite engineering methodology, and no program management processes to draw from," said Sam Araki, who joined Lockheed's Corona team in 1958 as a senior scientist and rose to become Lockheed's

The first Corona images of Plesetsk — one of Francis Gary Powers' targets during his ill-fated U-2 flight — revealed only four operational ICBMs. Still, this only stoked fears of potential Soviet ICBM sites not yet discovered.

"I HAVE DIRECTED PROMPT ATTENTION TO INCREASE OUR AIRLIFT CAPACITY. OBTAINING ADDITIONAL AIR TRANSPORT MOBILITY — AND OBTAINING IT NOW — WILL BETTER ASSURE THE ABILITY OF OUR CONVENTIONAL FORCES TO RESPOND, WITH DISCRIMINATION AND SPEED, TO ANY PROBLEM AT ANY SPOT ON THE GLOBE AT ANY MOMENT'S NOTICE."[3]

—PRESIDENT KENNEDY, STATE OF THE UNION ADDRESS, JANUARY 30, 1961

Missiles and Space Division President. "No one had ever done this before, and now we had less than a year to do what most people thought was impossible. We went through twelve major trial-and-error iterations to get everything right."[4]

Araki recounted the frenzied effort to invent, build and test some of America's first space-bound satellites from scratch: "We cobbled together components from machine shops and garages — early on, it was mostly auto parts — launched it into space and we learned as much as we could. The first time we launched, the film sublimated [instantly evaporated] when it was exposed to the vacuum of space. Lubricant sublimated, parts broke down, heat built up differently than we anticipated...but we looked at every failure as an opportunity to learn. It was our religion, and that's how we got it right."[5]

It wasn't easy, but the team launched the first successful Corona mission in just 24 months.

With 23 cockpit windows and high wings able to operate from rough fields, the original C-130 Hercules was the antithesis of the sleek, speedy jets of its day. It had a low center of gravity, reached 360 mph, and boasted a large, easily accessible cargo area that could carry 40,000 pounds. After more than 60 years of service, C-130 aircraft are still in production, providing unparalleled delivery and airdrop capabilities to civilian, military and humanitarian organizations worldwide.

A STRATEGIC ADVANTAGE: FLEET BALLISTIC MISSILES

As in any good chess match, the United States had to assume that its Soviet opponent might counter American reconnaissance strategies. The "bomber gap" and "missile gap" recon missions of the mid-1950s to early 1960s focused on the nuclear deployment capabilities of aircraft- and land-based weapon systems. But a land-based missile silo could be targeted, a bomber shot down. A roving fleet of nuclear-armed submarines offered the potential for a mobile and undetectable retaliation to a Soviet nuclear attack.

On December 17, 1955, representatives of several contractors gathered in Washington, D.C., for a briefing on a program to investigate the feasibility of converting ICBMs into submarine-launched weapons. This Fleet Ballistic Missile program aimed to introduce a profound strategic deterrent that could help keep the Cold War from heating up.

When Rear Adm. William Francis "Red" Raborn asked the gathered contractors to introduce themselves, Gene Root, director of corporate development planning and a champion of the recently created Missile Systems Division (a precursor to LMSD), was the first to stride confidently to the chalkboard. He wrote LOCKHEED in capital letters and turned to face the room.

"We're ready," Root said. "Who's next?"

Lockheed won the prime contract, which helped establish the Missile Systems Division. The hard work of Root's team paid off on July 20, 1960, with the successful first launch of the UGM-27 Polaris sea-launched ballistic missile from the USS *George Washington*. Less than five years had passed since that first meeting in Washington, and Lockheed's SLBM had become an integral part of the country's nuclear deterrence triad.

Over the coming decades, Lockheed worked with the U.S. Navy to refine and evolve its submarine-launched ballistic missiles, and the Polaris' range and warhead capability grew significantly. The British Navy was also equipped with Polaris missiles beginning with the A3 model in 1968, the final model of its line. The Fleet Ballistic Missile program helped establish Lockheed's location in Sunnyvale, and in 2006, Lockheed Martin opened its Fleet Ballistic Missile Post Production Center of Excellence at Cape Canaveral.

Underwater launches required different technologies from traditional land-based missiles. Compressed air streams ejected the missile from the submarine, and its first-stage engine ignited only when it was a safe distance above the sub. Then, an internal guidance system directed the weapon to the target.

Just as the U-2 dispelled the myth of the Soviet-U.S. "bomber gap" in the mid-1950s, Corona quelled concerns over a similar "missile gap." Imagery provided by this mission spanned more Soviet acreage than all previous U-2 overflights combined — which until that point had only covered about 14 percent of the heavily defended ICBM launch areas in the USSR — proving the value of orbital photo reconnaissance, and more importantly, keeping pilots and aircraft out of harm's way. Another mark of success: Corona's re-entry capsule became the first man-made artifact successfully recovered from orbit and set the stage for an intelligence revolution that spanned the coming decade. Despite its complexity, Corona had a run of 32 consecutive successful missions, including midair film recovery.

The limiting factors for Corona were its photographic resolution and breadth of coverage. It soon became clear that follow-on systems were needed that could provide data not only on the *number* of Soviet missiles in operation but also *how* these missiles were designed and manufactured. In building higher-resolution recon-naissance systems, engineers learned from the mistakes of Corona, emphasizing systems engineering and rigorous testing that mimicked the space environment. This long-term strategy paid dividends over the following decade, as did many forward-thinking investments made by U.S. leaders in the early 1960s.

ADDRESSING AIRLIFT MOBILITY

President John F. Kennedy promoted key space and missile programs that Eisenhower initiated, and also made air transport a core campaign issue. The Korean War had shown that U.S. aerial transports were ill-equipped for the kind of combat missions the military would face in the future. Some were too heavy. Some needed longer runways for takeoffs and landings. Others had weight restrictions, which prevented them from transporting bulky supplies or large numbers of soldiers. The United States needed a versatile aircraft that could be used for any and all transportation needs. Lockheed's C-130 Hercules accomplished precisely that.

Kelly Johnson was busy at the time developing the F-104 Starfighter and was generally more focused on high-performance fighter planes and reconnaissance aircraft than a utilitarian bird like the C-130. Hall Hibbard spearheaded the project, championing the work of engineer and project supervisor Willis Hawkins. Lockheed's design included four turboprop engines that provided the ability to pressurize the plane's fuselage, including the cargo compartment, allowing it to fly efficiently at high altitudes. The Air Force awarded the original C-130 contract to Lockheed in 1951, and in 1959 Congress directed the Air Force to further modernize its airlift capabilities, spurring a new generation of C-130s. An Air Force requirement for a new jet-powered strategic transport came in 1960. That project would become the C-141 StarLifter.

The StarLifter, produced on time and under budget, became the first production aircraft to be completely designed by engineers at the Lockheed-Georgia Company in Marietta, Ga., established in 1951. With Kennedy's support and the subsequent billion-dollar contract to produce 132 StarLifters, Marietta cemented itself as a major part of the Lockheed production arsenal.

Another far-reaching effect of the C-141 program was that it offered Lockheed the opportunity to make a bold choice in the burgeoning civil rights debate: It desegregated its Marietta operation. Lockheed's James Hodgson, who had worked with the company since 1941 and later served as U.S. Secretary of Labor, led the charge for this modernized workforce through a program later named Plan for Progress.

As stated in The New York Times, "Lockheed, which built many of America's most famous wartime and postwar aircraft, was one of the first big corporations to recruit and train black and Hispanic workers in the early 1960s. Mr. Hodgson promoted that program and a company plan that chipped in 50 cents for every dollar that workers invested in stocks or savings."[6] Lockheed CEO Robert Gross, too, supported these efforts, compelling Vice President and General Manager Dan Haughton to desegregate the Marietta facility "indirectly and with subtlety"[7] — a wise approach, given the social climate of the southern state and existing Georgia state law.

> The signs that had indicated segregated rest rooms and drinking fountains were quietly removed. Paper cups by the thousands were placed by all drinking fountains, and no one challenged the change. The segregated lunchrooms

The prototype YC-130 had a cargo deck that was capable of carrying an astonishing 300 pounds per square foot, lifted into the air after a ground roll of a mere 855 feet.

were simply abandoned. ... The indirect approach worked, not immediately but over time and without any upheaval. The percentage of black employees steadily increased, and black supervisors became increasingly common.[8]

More than 600 miles away at the White House, Kennedy pushed a button to open the hangar door at the rollout ceremony for the C-141. This event came almost exactly nine years to the day after Lockheed's YC-130 prototype was first flown. The investment in airlift capability would soon pay off: Both transport planes were soon deployed on critical missions throughout the world stemming from tumultuous turns during the first months of Kennedy's presidency.

This photo from the late 1970s shows the Lockheed C-141 StarLifter next to the "stretched" C-141B.

FROM THE EARTH TO THE MOON

On April 12, 1961, the Soviets shocked the world yet again by launching Russian cosmonaut Yuri Gagarin into orbital spaceflight. Another Soviet victory — the first man in space — could have been a devastating blow to the U.S. program. But less than a month later, Americans had a major triumph, sending Alan B. Shepard Jr. to an altitude of 117 miles before he safely landed in the ocean.

Kennedy harnessed this momentum to redefine the nascent space race:

> Now it is time to take longer strides — time for a great new American enterprise — time for this nation to take a clearly leading role in space achievement, which in many ways may hold the key to our future on Earth. ... I believe that this nation should commit itself to achieving the goal, before this decade is out, of landing a man safely on the moon and returning him safely to the Earth.[9]

Astronaut Gus Grissom achieved another suborbital flight like Shepard's on July 21, 1961. His success was marred, however, when his space capsule, the Liberty Bell 7, sank after splashdown (Grissom survived). Meanwhile, Russia's Gherman Titov became the first human to spend a full day in orbit and return safely. This technological sparring reached new heights on February 20, 1962, when John Glenn lifted off from Cape Canaveral in his Friendship 7 capsule atop an Atlas rocket.

Thirty seconds after liftoff, a guidance system locked on to a transponder in the Atlas booster and guided Glenn to space. Three minutes after launch, he got his first view of Earth's horizon from space. Two minutes later, Glenn's capsule separated from the Atlas booster, making John Glenn the first American to reach orbit.

ZERO DEFECTS

The "all systems go" successes of Glenn's mission, as well as the tough lessons of failures like Grissom's sunken space capsule, emphasized the importance of every component and every step of NASA's integrated spaceflight systems. During World War II aircraft design and production, minor defects were often tolerated to maintain

Spirited to space on an Atlas-Agena rocket (pictured at right), John Glenn traveled more than 75,000 miles in just under five hours, orbiting the planet three times. By the time he splashed down in the Atlantic Ocean later that same afternoon, he was a worldwide celebrity.

Martin Marietta's Baltimore Quality Control Manager Vernon Rawlings shares the podium with NASA's Gemini astronauts.

the speed of production lines. Multistage rockets, however, did not return to the hangar for repairs. The space age offered just one chance to get it right, and there was no room for error.

At the Orlando plant of Martin Marietta, which was formed in a merger of Martin and Chicago-based American Marietta Company in 1961, a far-reaching and influential program would soon be born: Zero Defects, the granddaddy of nearly every quality control program in the world. One of the plant's first jobs was the production of the first Pershing missile for the United States Army. Philip Crosby was the quality control manager on the Pershing missile program, and he established the four principles of Zero Defects:

WINNING PERSHING

On January 7, 1958, the Department of Defense had authorized the Army's Ballistic Missile Agency to develop a new solid-propellant nuclear missile to replace its aging Redstone missiles. The request for proposal was sent to seven firms. Most came before the selection board with complex slides and detailed handouts. One — the Martin company — came with only a piece of chalk and a few brilliant ideas.

Martin's proposal manager Sid Stark drew a missile with a sharply pointed warhead and outlined a design that could be easily transported by helicopter or aircraft, durable enough to withstand extreme weather conditions, and capable of being fired at a moment's notice by a squadron of well-trained soldiers. Ed Uhl, a member of the proposal team, added a key incentive. Imagine, Uhl said, the cost savings of assembling the missile in Orlando and then transporting it just 50 miles down the road to Cape Canaveral for testing. Uhl received a phone call on March 22, 1958, informing him that Martin had won the contract for the Pershing missile system.

Pershing ballistic missile on its launcher, 1958.

1. Quality is conformance to requirements
2. Defect prevention is preferable to quality inspection and correction
3. Zero Defects is the quality standard
4. Quality is measured in monetary terms — the Price of Nonconformance

Crosby's standards were credited with a 25 percent reduction in the Pershing missile program's overall rejection rate and a 30 percent reduction in scrap costs. Martin Marietta offered Zero Defects freely to all other aerospace companies, and years later, it was adopted by automobile manufacturers around the world, as well.

COMMUNISM IN CUBA

The stage was set for the next great push into the unknown. Martin's diversification into missile systems had paid off in spades, with contracts to develop the Vanguard, the Titan and the Pershing missile system. While the newly merged Martin Marietta, which employed 56,000 people in 48 states and 13 countries, answered the country's call for advanced missile systems, Lockheed served one of Kennedy's other national priorities: addressing the spread of communism.

Only days after Gagarin's historic spaceflight in 1961, a badly mismanaged invasion of Cuba by CIA-supported Cuban exiles failed to eradicate the communist regime established in 1959 by Fidel Castro. At the time, Laos was another hot spot of communist growth, but with the failure of the Bay of Pigs invasion in Cuba, Kennedy was hesitant to launch a similar offensive in Southeast Asia.

Kennedy met with Khrushchev at the Vienna Summit on June 4, 1961, to discuss the neutrality of Laos and lay the groundwork for the building of the Berlin Wall. Unknown to the Russian leader, that same month, the first of 15 U.S. Jupiter nuclear missiles capable of quickly hitting the Soviet Union were deployed to Turkey.

As Turkey — a NATO ally — became a strategic location for the United States, Castro's claim in July 1962 of massive Soviet support made U.S. military leaders view Cuba as a similar proxy for the USSR. To assess the threat, Kennedy soon called on Lockheed's stalwart reconnaissance systems: the U-2 reconnaissance aircraft and the Corona photoreconnaissance satellite.

A Lockheed P2V Neptune patrols a Soviet freighter attempting to carry IL-28 aircraft into Cuba, 1962.

MRBM FIELD LAUNCH SITE
SAN CRISTOBAL NO 1
14 OCTOBER 1962

ERECTOR/LAUNCHER EQUIPMENT

TENT AREAS

EQUIPMENT

ERECTOR/LAUNCHER EQUIPMENT

8 MISSILE TRAILERS

CONSTRUCTIO

Lockheed U-2 photos of Cuban missile installations shown to Kennedy on October 16, 1962.

The U-2 had ceased overflights of the Soviet Union after the Powers incident, but the CIA had been using the U-2 to observe Cuba for years. On October 14, 1962, a U-2 piloted by Maj. Richard Heyser gathered hard evidence of Soviet ballistic missile installations in Cuba capable of striking the United States.

Over the next 13 days, U-2 flights would keep Kennedy and his advisers abreast of Soviet activity in Cuba. When U-2 pilot Maj. Rudolph Anderson was shot down over Cuba by a Soviet-supplied surface-to-air missile, tensions reached a fever pitch, but Kennedy opted for a naval blockade of Cuba, enforced by maritime patroller aircraft like the Lockheed P2V Neptune and the brand-new Orion P-3, rather than an all-out strike. The blockade bought the Kennedy administration enough time to negotiate a deal with the Soviets: Russia would dismantle its weapons in Cuba in exchange for a pledge by the United States not to invade the island, pulling both sides from the brink of nuclear war.

SR-71 production line in Burbank, 1960s.

THE EVOLUTION OF RECONNAISSANCE

The stalemate of the Cuban Missile Crisis illustrated the efficacy of the nuclear deterrent-based foreign policy suggested by George Kennan in the aftermath of World War II: The *threat* of global annihilation by nuclear war had saved the world.

Still, the loss of Anderson — the only person killed by enemy fire during the Cuban Missile Crisis — showed that even the high-flying U-2 was vulnerable to ever-improving anti-aircraft technology. The military asked Lockheed for another "impossible" technology: an aircraft that could not be shot down. The speed of the new aircraft was to exceed 2,000 mph. Other planes of the era could, in theory, approximate that speed, but only in short, afterburner-driven bursts. This new plane needed to maintain record speed for hours at a time. At such velocity, friction with the atmosphere generates temperatures that would melt a conventional airframe.

"EVERYTHING ABOUT THE AIRCRAFT HAD TO BE INVENTED."

— KELLY JOHNSON

"Everything about the aircraft had to be invented." Kelly Johnson recalled.[10]

Titanium alloy was the only option for the airframe — as strong as stainless steel but relatively lightweight and durable at high temperatures. Skunk Works' Ben Rich spent untold hours tackling the problem of how heat could be distributed across the entire airframe. Then he recalled a simple lesson from one of his university courses: Black paint both emits and absorbs heat. The aircraft was painted black and earned the name Blackbird.

The original Blackbird made its first flight on April 30, 1962. Setting records nearly every time it flew, the Blackbird achieved a sustained speed above Mach 3 on July 20, 1963, at an astounding altitude of 78,000 feet. Piloting the Blackbird was an unforgiving endeavor, demanding total concentration. But pilots were eager to fly the fastest bird on record.

"It was almost a religious experience," said Air Force Col. Jim Wadkins. "Nothing had prepared me to fly that fast."[11]

By the mid-1960s, Lockheed's Skunk Works employed nearly 8,000 workers to deliver one Blackbird per month. The SR-71 Blackbird entered service in January 1966, and it began two decades of deployment on mission-critical reconnaissance missions, setting numerous world aviation records for speed and altitude in the process. Even today, it remains the world's fastest and highest-flying manned aircraft and holds the distinction of having never been shot down by any anti-aircraft or missile defense system.

Just as the SR-71 Blackbird served as a new generation of reconnaissance aircraft building on the U-2, Lockheed's KH-8 satellite, code-named Gambit, built upon the early success of its Corona satellites.

With aircraft zipping across the sky at 3,000 feet per second, the rules of navigation needed to be rewritten. Visual references for conventional flying — highways, rivers and metropolitan areas — were rendered obsolete, giving way to mountain ranges, coastlines and large bodies of water.

The Gambit KH-7 spy satellite took high-resolution photos of the Soviet Plesetsk ICBM launch complex in June 1967.

GAMBIT'S SHARP EYE

While Corona was still operational, the National Reconnaissance Office launched a new spy satellite in 1963. Called Gambit, it covered less area than Corona, but it produced images at a higher resolution. Objects smaller than two feet could now be identified.

Also developed in a short 24 months, Gambit 3's unprecedented resolution meant intelligence analysts could more accurately identify and count individual vehicles, planes and ships — a major step forward in assessing the Soviets' true military strength. With precise knowledge of Soviet capabilities, U.S. strategists could design smarter and more effective defensive plans and systems.

As the United States got a greater visual handle on its Cold War adversary, however, another proxy war was heating up under the jungle canopies of Southeast Asia.

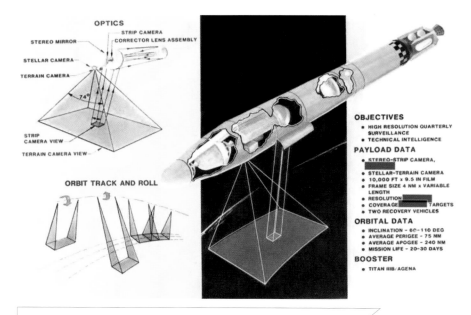

Launched on an Atlas-Agena rocket, the Gambit reconnaissance satellite used an upgraded KH-7 camera system employing three separate cameras.

Equipped with ground-target radar, 20 mm Gatling guns, 40 mm cannons, and later, a side-firing 105 mm Howitzer, C-130s morphed into AC-130 gunships, destroying 10,000 enemy trucks and repelling countless enemy attacks in Vietnam. Late in the war, Hercules planes were even being fitted with the largest bomb in the U.S. arsenal, the 15,000-pound BLU-82.

VIETNAM AIR TRANSPORTS

Nothing had prepared the nation for the dark yet transformative era that was to follow the Cuban Missile Crisis. After narrowly averting nuclear war, the United States found itself once again mired in the reality of traditional warfare — this time in Vietnam. After Kennedy's assassination in November 1963, a massive escalation of the war in Southeast Asia began. As with the war in Korea in the early 1950s, the goal was to prevent the communist North from taking over South Vietnam without provoking war with China or the Soviet Union.

By 1965, the numbers of troops and aerial support vehicles deployed grew exponentially. Transport aircraft like the Lockheed C-130 Hercules and C-141 StarLifter were immediately pressed into service in Vietnam, delivering soldiers and supplies.

As the war progressed, C-130s were modified into MC-130 Combat Talons, which could pick up Special Operations forces in hostile territories and act as flying fuel tankers, orbiting in the sky as American rescue helicopters connected with them to refuel.

C-141s, meanwhile, cut flying time from California to Saigon and back from 95 hours to just 34. The most famous StarLifter missions involved repatriation of American prisoners of war back to the United States in 1973, transporting 588 POWs back to the United States, and playing an important role in rescuing American personnel and Vietnamese refugees during the 1975 evacuation of Saigon. Despite the value of the C-130 and C-141, the U.S. military needed an even larger military transport that could carry heavy tanks and helicopters any place in the world.

C-130s were perfectly equipped to carry out low-altitude parachute extraction drops of cargo, which led to the plane's key role in the defense of Khe Sanh in 1968. C-130s accounted for 90 percent of the supplies used by troops defending the village against the North Vietnamese siege.

Lockheed won the competition to develop and build this super-sized transport in 1965. The requirements were daunting. The transport needed a maximum takeoff weight more than twice that of the C-141. When Lockheed delivered the first C-5 Galaxy to the U.S. Air Force in 1970, it was one of the world's largest military aircraft, with a cargo compartment five times as large as that of the C-141 — big enough to hold four Sheridan light tanks or a Chinook helicopter. Almost immediately, the plane took off for Vietnam. Because it could transport about 98 percent of the Army's range of equipment, the C-5 Galaxy soon became indispensable to the war effort.

In addition to these transport aircraft, reconnaissance aircraft were deployed to Vietnam, as well. Lockheed EC-121 Constellations were flown in elliptical orbit over enemy territory to collect and transmit information on air activity. Meanwhile, Martin engineers had created upgraded reconnaissance and attack versions of their B-57 Canberra aircraft in the mid-1950s. By the time the B-57s were called into combat in 1964, Martin Marietta engineers had versions painted with the standard three-color Vietnam camouflage. Other variants employed night-reflecting paint, night optics, a new bubble cockpit and ejection seats. Many versions were nimble

ENTER AEGIS

Away from Vietnam, with Russian and American submarines and battleships carefully jockeying for position across the globe, another highly maneuverable enemy missile was designed to skim just above water, evading radar while locking on to seaborne targets. The devastating new technology debuted on Oct. 21, 1967, when an Egyptian gunship fired four Russian-built Styx missiles at the Israeli warship *Eliat*. The missiles streaked toward their target, impervious to counter-measures, sinking the *Eliat* and killing 47 of its crew.

For years, the Navy had studied various combinations of radar, armor and onboard missile systems to protect its ships at sea. It was time to develop a new defense system — a system that, in time, would become the most effective defender ever put to sea. Originally named the Advanced Surface Missile System, the Navy's new initiative called for the creation of an onboard

defensive missile system capable of detecting and inter-cepting incoming missiles launched from air and sea. Renamed Aegis in homage to the magical shield used by Zeus, the program launched in 1969 with Lockheed Martin heritage company RCA (later GE Aerospace) as lead contractor.

Unlike conventional rotating radar of the period, which gauged the speed and direction of a target once every 10 to 30 seconds, Aegis was designed to lock on to multiple incoming missiles and aircraft, continuously tracking their movements while assigning each a potential threat value. Once fixed on a target, the system relayed the oncoming missile's position back to the ship's main computer and helped crew members quickly and decisively calculate how to best intercept it and select defensive countermeasures.

Lockheed Martin has supported the Navy's Aegis system for more than four decades. This effort includes wide-ranging, detailed involvement in all combat systems to ensure an integrated, fast reacting, war-ready ship system.

Radio-controlled bombs were shown to be relatively inaccurate. The Walleye system represented a great leap forward, making automatic course corrections during descent and increasing accuracy.

enough for low-level attacks yet sturdy enough to deliver bombs from high altitudes, and the Canberra became the first aircraft to successfully target Viet Cong outposts in the Republic of South Vietnam in 1965. The EB-57s were later used for electronic reconnaissance missions.

Guided munitions, or "smart" bombs and missiles, also made their debut in Vietnam. In the early years of the war, the Martin Marietta AGM-12 Bullpup was the military's primary air-to-ground guided missile. Using a radio guidance system, pilots could manually steer these missiles toward their targets using a small joystick. By early 1967, an upgraded version of this system called the AGM-62 Walleye added a tiny television camera to the nose of an unpowered glide bomb. Scanning the ground below from its wing-mounted position, the Walleye's camera sent an image of the target to a pilot's TV screen, enabling them to "lock on" to a specific mark and fire. Once the missile was launched, an onboard guidance system made course corrections to direct the missile accurately to its target, ushering in a new age of precision-guidance technologies.

The USS Norton Sound became the first ship-borne test bed for the new Aegis Combat System, c. 1973.

A B-57B Canberra, upgraded and camouflaged for operations in Vietnam, emits smoke during a normal cartridge-starting procedure. Only 36 B-57s, many of them unpainted, were used in Vietnam, 1968.

REACHING THE FINISH LINE

Despite Cold War tensions and the conflict in Southeast Asia, the race to the moon continued unabated. In the mid-1960s, NASA's Gemini program proved an important bridge between the one-man Mercury missions and Apollo's lunar landing ambitions. To help protect the Gemini astronauts during the critical and dangerous launch phase, Martin Marietta's Titan launch vehicles included built-in systems that would shut down a launch if they encountered a problem.

The system was put to the test on December 12, 1965. Gemini astronauts Wally Schirra and Tom Stafford lay on their backs in the Gemini capsule, pointed to the sky. Beneath them, the Titan booster contained a quarter-million pounds of highly volatile rocket fuel. When the countdown hit zero, the engines fired and the astronauts prepared for launch. But the Malfunction Detection System discovered that an umbilical tail plug had prematurely fallen out of the rocket, and it automatically interrupted the launch before a potentially fatal liftoff. It was the only instance in which a launch was halted because of a malfunction — a testament to the success of the Zero Defects manufacturing approach. The Gemini VI-A successfully launched three days later, achieving the first manned rendezvous with another spacecraft, its sister ship Gemini VII.

In 1965 and 1966, the Titan-launched Gemini program successfully placed 10 pairs of astronauts in orbit, perfecting rendezvous techniques while studying the human impact of prolonged spaceflight. The finish line was finally in sight, but it would take the combined efforts of thousands of men and women to accomplish its ultimate goal: putting a man on the moon.

American hopes of reaching the moon were pinned on Project Apollo. Many companies were contracted to contribute to the Apollo program, including the Lockheed Propulsion Company, which designed and built the solid propellant launch escape motor and the pitch control motor for the spacecraft. These manned capsules were to be launched by powerful Saturn multistage rockets designed by von Braun's team. With the start of Apollo and its Soviet counterpart Zond program, the race to the moon reached its zenith.

The Russian bid to get there first depended on the success of the massive N-1 rocket, the answer to the Saturn V launch vehicle. A series of disastrous launches and explosions of the Soviet N-1 Moon rocket left the door open for the American space program to reach the finish line first.

It was July 20, 1969, and, again, the cameras were rolling. Some 530 million viewers watched a televised image of Neil Armstrong and heard him describe, via live audio, Apollo 11 touching down on the moon. With astronaut Michael Collins piloting the command module, Armstrong and Buzz Aldrin were the first people to set foot on the lunar landscape, cementing the historic moment with the immortal words, "That's one small step for man, one giant leap for mankind."

Simply setting foot on the moon was only part of the task ahead. Set for a July 24 splashdown in the Pacific Ocean, the Apollo 11 crew still faced the dangerous Earth re-entry phase.

At Hickam Air Force Base in Hawaii, Capt. Hank Brandli, a weather tracker and prediction specialist, used data from weather satellites to support the top-secret Corona program. While performing his typical duties in support of Corona drops, he discovered that the Apollo 11 astronauts were scheduled to re-enter the atmosphere directly in the path of a vicious thunderstorm that, according to Brandli, "would have ripped their parachutes to shreds. Without parachutes, they'd have crashed into the ocean with a force that would have killed them instantly. I was the only person who knew this and, because the program and its technology were strictly classified, I couldn't warn NASA."[12]

Brandli alerted Navy Capt. Willard "Sam" Huston Jr., who had the authority to persuade the government to reroute the entire naval fleet of Apollo 11 support carriers to a new splashdown location. Eleventh-hour changes were also made to the capsule's re-entry plan.

One small step for man, 1969.

At 195 hours, three minutes flight time, the Apollo 11 command module re-entered the atmosphere, its heat shield melting away as planned into white-hot plasma, blocking communication between the command center and the crew of astronauts plummeting toward Earth. At 195 hours, 15 minutes, the recovery carrier USS *Hornet* reported a sonic boom and reestablished communication with Armstrong. At 195 hours, 17 minutes, the *Hornet* confirmed the parachutes had deployed. One minute later, splashdown. As soon as Armstrong, Aldrin and Collins were safely aboard the *Hornet*, it was official: America had risen to the challenge and beaten Kennedy's deadline with months to spare. The space race had been won.

Once travel to distant worlds was a reality, an infinite frontier lay before humanity. Lockheed, Martin and a few billion stargazers worldwide prepared for the possibility of exploring these outer realms and unlocking the secrets of space.

The lunar module Eagle ascends toward the command module Columbia on July 21, 1969. In the background, the Earth rise is visible above the lunar horizon.

CHAPTER 6

CLEAN ROOMS

Breaking Down Barriers
1970–1990

"SINCE THE EARLIEST DAYS OF ASTRONOMY,
SINCE THE TIME OF GALILEO, ASTRONOMERS
HAVE SHARED A SINGLE GOAL — TO SEE MORE,
SEE FARTHER, SEE DEEPER."[1]

—HUBBLE SPACE TELESCOPE

MAKING SPACE WORK

They assembled it piece by piece, but everything had to work together, a unified whole. The project would take more than 20 years to come to fruition, but beginning in the early 1970s, Lockheed Missiles and Space Company engineers began building a full-scale mockup for what would become the Hubble Space Telescope. This school-bus-sized, solar-powered orbiter would one day give humanity its first-ever unobstructed view of the cosmos.

The 1.3 million cubic feet of space in Lockheed's high bay clean room was used in the construction and integration of the Hubble Space Telescope. [INSET] The Viking 1 Mars lander spacecraft is assembled in a Martin Marietta Aerospace clean room in Denver, Colo., 1974.

Martin Marietta's rocket-powered X-24A lifting body research vehicle is fixed under the wing of a B-52 mother ship, preparing for a test flight, c. 1970.

Though Hubble promised to be the largest and most powerful scientific instrument ever deployed in space, the devil was in the details, and even a minute blemish on the delicate instrumentation could derail the collaborative aerospace effort. The world's largest clean room offered a highly controlled environment that used sophisticated vacuum technology to filter contaminants out of the air. "If you get dust on the mirror, you get scattering of light," said Lockheed's Domenick Tenerelli, chief systems engineer on the Hubble Space Telescope.[2] But the ill effects of tiny dust particles were only part of the challenge.

Hubble was built to be upgraded and serviced by astronauts, and its ride to orbit would be aboard NASA's new Space Transportation System — the space shuttle. With a recession looming, the days of expendable spacecraft were over. For space exploration to be remotely cost-effective, the space shuttle would merge the launch power of reusable rockets with the maneuverability of airplanes, so it could complete a round-trip flight to space and land safely on a runway, ready for future use.

On March 19, 1970, a massive B-52 took off from Edwards Air Force Base with a flat-bellied, wingless aircraft tucked snugly under its wing. This was the Martin Marietta X-24A "lifting body" spaceplane, the progenitor of the modern space shuttle. At an altitude of 40,000 feet, the B-52 dropped this single vehicle into the blue sky. The X-24A descended in free fall until its pilot, Jerauld Gentry, ignited a rocket engine, propelling the silver teardrop-shaped vehicle high into the sky at speeds approaching Mach 1. Gentry then allowed the aircraft to descend sharply toward the ground, where he performed an unpowered landing on a dry lake bed.

Gentry's feat proved what many scientists had thought impossible: that a wingless aircraft could descend from the upper atmosphere and glide safely back to Earth. If the same aerodynamic principles could be applied to a larger spacecraft capable of carrying astronaut crews and heavy payloads into space and back, it might be possible to place complex instruments such as Hubble into orbit.

Following the climactic space race of the 1960s, the aerospace industry next aimed to establish a consistent and working human presence in space. Satellites continued to gather scientific data and military intelligence, but distant planets and the deeper reaches of space called out for exploration. The volatile economy of the 1970s and '80s made reusable spacecraft and more permanent space stations vital. Meanwhile, Soviet and U.S. governments chose sides in the Middle East, Asia and Latin America — new hotboxes acting as proxies for the ongoing Cold War. Dynamic changes in global politics and economies demanded unprecedented levels of cooperation for global leaders to move past old rivalries and for explorers to reach beyond the moon.

AFTER ARMSTRONG

Apollo 11 had captivated millions, the eyes of the world watching man's age-old quest reach its destination and apparent conclusion. For some, however, the heroic feat accomplished by NASA and its partners was only the beginning of a new era of discovery. With moon landings achieved, the next frontier would be to establish a more permanent working environment in space — a place to pursue scientific advancement and further humanity's understanding of the universe.

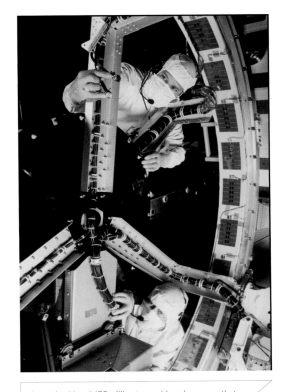

It cost Lockheed $30 million to provide a clean room that would ensure that Hubble's optics and instruments were free of dust, filtering out particles as small as 1/50th the width of a human hair.

"THOSE WHO WOULD BE OUR ADVERSARIES, WE INVITE TO A PEACEFUL COMPETITION — NOT IN CONQUERING TERRITORY OR EXTENDING DOMINION, BUT IN ENRICHING THE LIFE OF MAN. AS WE EXPLORE THE REACHES OF SPACE, LET US GO TO THE NEW WORLDS TOGETHER — NOT AS NEW WORLDS TO BE CONQUERED, BUT AS A NEW ADVENTURE TO BE SHARED."[3]

—PRESIDENT NIXON, INAUGURAL ADDRESS, 1969

The famous "blue marble" image of Earth taken on Apollo 17, the final lunar mission, 1972.

By repurposing hardware from their planned lunar missions, the Soviets successfully launched the world's first space station, Salyut 1, on April 19, 1971. The purpose of the Salyut series was to establish a stable hub for experimentation, with more comfortable accommodations that allowed astronauts to spend more time in space. Sadly, the program was punctuated by tragedy in the summer of 1971 when a returning Soviet spacecraft depressurized and three cosmonauts died upon re-entry into the Earth's atmosphere.

America's first space station was Skylab, which was created from the repurposed third stage of a Saturn V rocket. In January 1972, Martin Marietta won the contract to support Skylab space station launch operations, assembling and conducting prelaunch testing of the docking adapters used to rendezvous with the transport spacecraft. Skylab launched on May 14, 1973.

The crews that occupied this comparatively roomy "Orbital Workshop" — containing sleeping quarters, kitchen, dining area, bathroom and shower — now shifted from the test pilot astronauts of the Mercury, Gemini and Apollo eras to include scientist-astronauts capable of conducting useful research in space.

Beginning in 1973, Skylab astronaut crews lived and worked in a large space laboratory for periods of 28 to 56 days. Developed by Martin Marietta Denver Aerospace, the Multiple Docking Adapter functioned as garage, entry hall and observatory. This horizontal cutaway shows the narrowed end for docking and entrance.

While Skylab provided a scientific outpost in space, the concept of the so-called space shuttle would become a reality with President Richard Nixon's official blessing in January 1972. The winning shuttle design included two reusable rocket boosters, an expendable external fuel tank and a central orbiter — part rocket, part crew and cargo space plane. Martin Marietta was selected to build the massive external tank, the structural backbone of all future shuttle flights.

As humanity moved ever closer to establishing a stable work environment in space, a series of upheavals destabilized various regions back on Earth.

TERRORISM & TREATIES

Myriad violent conflicts signaled unrest around the world in the late 1960s and early '70s from the Middle East to Southeast Asia. These conflicts arose amid a shift in Cold War tensions. The Nuclear Non-Proliferation Treaty among the United Kingdom, United States, Soviet Union and numerous other countries went into effect in March 1970. Soon after, the Strategic Arms Limitation Talks and subsequent Anti-Ballistic Missile Treaty between the two Cold War superpowers, first signed in 1972 by President Nixon and Soviet General Secretary Leonid Brezhnev, aimed to regulate offensive and defensive missile systems.

The United States continued its surveillance of Soviet missile installations, ensuring the sanctity of the agreement between the two countries. With precise knowledge of Soviet capabilities, U.S. strategists could design smarter and more effective defensive plans and systems. While reconnaissance satellites such as Lockheed's Gambit and Hexagon helped the United States keep watch over the Soviet Union, Skunk Works conceived a new type of aircraft that might prove invisible to enemy eyes.

THE INVISIBLE MAN

In the summer of 1972, Ben Rich, one of the most renowned engineers in Lockheed's Skunk Works division, stood nervously outside the office of his boss, Kelly Johnson. In the 18 years since Rich joined Skunk Works, the two men had developed a close mentor-protégé relationship.

Ben Rich, Kelly Johnson's successor as head of Skunk Works. Rich had helped his mentor shore up thermodynamic and propulsion issues with some of his most famous creations, including the SR-71 Blackbird.

Rich had come to tell Johnson that he'd been offered a new position at a rival manufacturer. Johnson listened, shook his head and shared his own secret: In three years, he would be retiring. And when he did, he planned to recommend Rich as the new Skunk Works director, arguably the most prestigious engineering post in aviation. Rich stayed. And Johnson delivered on his promise, helping his protégé win the post he not only desired but also deserved. With a redesign of the division's famed U-2 spy plane in early 1975 to meet contemporary mission requirements and to make the Dragon Lady fly better, Rich's Skunk Works team quickly won over the Pentagon.

With Soviet anti-air defenses growing more capable every year, U.S. Defense Department officials began looking for a way to make aircraft essentially invisible. Despite success with the U-2 and SR-71, Lockheed initially wasn't invited to join the competition to build an attack aircraft undetectable by enemy radar. Rich, with Johnson's help, worked Lockheed into the competition.

HEXAGON'S BROAD LOOK

Lockheed's Corona satellite put eyes in space. In 1963, the Gambit program provided superior resolution. The next-generation system was born in 1971. Called Hexagon, it was developed under the auspices of the NRO by the Air Force, the CIA and Lockheed's Sunnyvale team to combine Corona's wide-ranging reach with Gambit's sharp resolution. At 10 feet in diameter and 67 feet in length, it's not surprising that the press nicknamed the 30,000-pound unacknowledged satellite *Big Bird*.

Armed with all of the lessons learned from Corona, the Hexagon team built an exquisite testing infrastructure that re-created the harsh environment of space on the ground. A large acoustic chamber mimicked the powerful thrust of rocket boosters. A huge thermal vacuum chamber simulated the deep space environment for satellite orbital testing. The program office, development and test facilities were consolidated into one building so the entire satellite could be designed, built and tested in one place.

The testing procedures and technologies built by the Hexagon team were so advanced they propelled Hexagon to a record of no satellite failures. In fact, many of the same facilities used to test Hexagon are still in use today.

Hexagon's first flight lasted 52 days, and it had a 500-pound load of film in each of its four film capsules, compared to the 40- to 160-pound loads the Corona vehicles carried. Within weeks, Hexagon would be able to photograph nearly the entirety of the Soviet Union in such detail that analysts would be able to count and identify Soviet missile silos in operation or under construction. On many of its later missions, Hexagon also carried a separate camera for high-fidelity mapping. There were 19 successful launches of Hexagon satellites in a reconnaissance career that stretched from 1971 to 1986.

Corona, Gambit and Hexagon were more than just techno-logical marvels. Between 1960 and 1986, they provided seven presidents with critical intelligence about the Soviet Union. At a time when the world was holding its breath at the prospect of nuclear war, these groundbreaking satellites gave America's leaders crucial insight into the true capabilities of the Soviet military and confirmed their acquiescence to the eventual nuclear détente agreements. That intelligence helped prevent heated tensions from boiling over, settled "missile gap" questions, confirmed compliance with nuclear arms limitation agreements and supported the peaceful end of the Cold War.

Despite the technological advances from Corona to Gambit to Hexagon, dropping film capsules from space had some obvious limitations. A re-entry capsule's parachute failed after being dropped from the first Hexagon satellite and sank to the bottom of the Pacific Ocean, some 16,000 feet underwater (it was retrieved in April 1972). The growing need for real-time image transfer hastened the transition from film to digital imaging.

Rich turned to a pair of young engineers, Denys Overholser and Dick Sherrer, who developed a computer program based on the theory that radar beams could be reflected by a series of carefully angled triangular panels.

Two years later, the resulting blueprints — dubbed the "Hopeless Diamond" by naysayers — were converted into a wooden model that was mounted on a pole and exposed to radar from every angle to see just how visible it was. Early tests showed that the aircraft registered no bigger than an ordinary marble and thus was nearly impossible to detect. In response, Rich, ever the savvy salesman, brought a bag of ball bearings to the Pentagon and rolled a few across a general's desk, saying, "Here's the observability of your airplane on radar."[4]

Lockheed won the contract in 1976 to begin work on Have Blue, the stealth demonstrator that would lead to the F-117A Nighthawk.

The Have Blue program confirmed that radar signatures low enough to negate battlefield air defense threats could be achieved in a practical flight vehicle. Two aircraft were developed in the mid-1970s, complemented by the development of the first practical computer program, Echo 1, which accurately predicted the radar signature of an air vehicle. The Have Blue program led to the development of the successful F-117A.

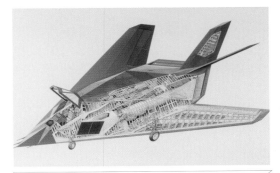

Denys Overholser and Dick Sherrer's computer program had revealed that a diamond-shaped aircraft — what looked on paper like a flying engagement ring — would be 1,000 times less visible to radar than any other aircraft ever created at Lockheed. The flat surfaces, sharp edges and tilted facets of the F-117A's design reflected radar signals away at odd angles, while specially created surface materials absorbed radar energy.

LOCKHEED'S LAST AIRLINER

In April 1972, after six grueling years of design modifications and unanticipated delays in engine development, Lockheed delivered to Eastern Airlines the most technologically advanced commercial jet of its era, the L-1011 TriStar. Going head to head with the Douglas DC-10 aircraft, the new airliner represented Lockheed's bid to re-establish itself in the commercial aviation market after a series of failures in the early 1960s.

Similar to countless other iconic aircraft before it, the L-1011 faced daunting technical challenges on the way to its inaugural flight. Additionally, financial difficulties ravaged its engine manufacturer, and a recession fueled by the world's first oil crisis in the Middle East decreased demand for commercial flights. Nevertheless, in 1972, Eastern Airlines began scheduled service of the L-1011.

On the runway, the Lockheed L-1011 TriStar was an undeniable beauty. But in flight, the L-1011 was nothing short of a miracle. On May 25, 1972, veteran test pilots Anthony LeVier and Charles Hall transported 115 crew members, employees and reporters on a four-hour, 13-minute flight from Palmdale, Calif.,

to Dulles International Airport outside Washington, D.C., with the TriStar's advanced electronic fly-by-wire automatic flight control system engaged from takeoff to landing.

It was a groundbreaking moment: the first cross-country flight without the need for human hands on the controls. Fly-by-wire technology was here to stay.

Early TriStar customers included Air Canada, ANA, British Airways, TWA, Cathay Pacific, Gulf Air, Saudia and the operator with the largest fleet, Delta. Unfortunately, the supplier-developed engines continued to experience problems. Annual program losses mounted, totaling nearly $650 million over a five-year period in the late 1970s. Although a technological marvel, the L-1011 was a financial failure.

In a difficult decision designed to minimize losses, the company shut down production of the L-1011 in 1981, and the last of 250 aircraft was delivered in 1982. Still, Lockheed exited commercial aviation having created, in one pilot's words, "the most intelligent airliner ever to fly."[5]

With its large, curved nose, low-set wings and graceful swept tail, the L-1011 looked as sleek as a dolphin. Conceived during the mid-1960s to transport 250 passengers on popular transcontinental routes, the L-1011 boasted unheard-of luxuries, including glare-resistant windows, full-sized hideaway closets for coats and a below-deck galley, which lifted filet mignon and lamb chop dinners up to the main cabin via two elevators.

AIRLIFTS ABOUND

While Skunk Works dove into development of the fighter aircraft of the future, several air transport mainstays in the Lockheed fleet were called into service yet again. In October 1973, on the Jewish high holiday of Yom Kippur, Egypt and Syria attacked the Golan Heights. Israel was caught by surprise and quickly exhausted its defense munitions. With the very real threat of nuclear escalation, Prime Minister Golda Meir made a plea for military support, but NATO countries initially chose to stay out of the conflict. This changed when it became clear that the Soviet Union was resupplying the aggressor.

Two Lockheed transports played a critical role in ensuring Israel did not fall to enemy forces. Nixon authorized a massive U.S. resupply effort on October 13, deploying Lockheed C-141 StarLifters and C-5 Galaxy heavy-lift transport aircraft to Israel in an effort dubbed Operation Nickel Grass. No aircraft other than the Galaxy was large enough to transport the tanks, helicopters and ammunition that Israel needed. Vital cargo rolled out of Lockheed's planes by the ton.

"For generations to come," Meir said, "all will be told of the miracle of the immense planes from the United States."[6]

Transport aircraft also provided significant airlift support in the final months of the Vietnam War. The C-141 dramatically reduced the amount of time it took to transport those with injuries to hospitals in the United States.

Following Nixon's resignation, and with support for the war at an all-time low, North Vietnamese forces launched a major offensive on the South. As a chaotic South Vietnamese retreat took place, it became clear that Saigon would soon fall to the enemy. Beginning on April 21, 1975, C-141s and C-130s began an extensive round-the-clock evacuation. In only a month's time, fleets of the two Lockheed aircraft were responsible for airlifting more than 45,000 people out of Saigon, including more than 5,600 U.S. citizens.[7] By May 1975, the airlifts were over, officially ending America's involvement in Vietnam.

An M60 tank is unloaded from a C-5 Galaxy during Operation Nickel Grass. In one month, from October 14 to November 14, 1973, C-141s flew 421 missions to Israel, delivering 11,632 tons of equipment and supplies. C-5s flew 145 missions and delivered 10,673 tons of supplies.

Former U.S. POWs cheer after taking off from Hanoi, North Vietnam, in a Lockheed C-141 StarLifter in 1973 as part of Operation Homecoming. In 1975, some 12,000 people were brought out of Tan Son Nhut Air Base outside of Saigon aboard C-130s and C-141s. They also transported some 31,000 refugees from the Philippines to Guam.

BIRTH OF THE FIGHTING FALCON

Conceived in the early 1970s by a small but vocal group of engineers and defense analysts known as the Lightweight Fighter Mafia, the F-16 represented a major change in fighter design. Its fine blend of technology and commonsense requirements emphasized flight performance — range, persistence and maneuverability — right in the heart of the flight envelope where air combat takes place. The aircraft's user-friendly cockpit and integrated avionic system allowed a single pilot to fight and win in aerial combat. The design also emphasized low cost in procurement, operation and support, and provisions for growth.

Beginning in 1975, the YF-16 design team at the General Dynamics Forth Worth division (which Lockheed would acquire in 1993) translated those ideas into the most advanced combat platform of its day: the Fighting Falcon. In the wake of recent Middle Eastern conflicts, the Air Force wanted the Lightweight Fighter to be able to bomb enemy installations and win dogfights, as well. After winning a flyoff against the rival YF-17 (which became the Navy's F/A-18 Hornet), engineers at Fort Worth added more powerful weapons and targeting systems without diminishing the F-16's unparalleled agility, transforming the Fighting Falcon into a true multirole aircraft.

The F-16's smooth blended-wing body provided extra lift and control; its fly-by-wire system increased agility; and its side-mounted throttle, head-up display, and bubble-top canopy improved visibility and control, 1980s.

OBSERVATION AND EXPLORATION

As the Vietnam War ended and the immediate evacuation and airlift needs decreased, one special C-141 StarLifter saw new life. Originally built as a commercial variant of the military airlifter, the lone L-300 was sold to NASA and converted into the Kuiper Airborne Observatory. This highly modified aircraft provided NASA with a new platform for astronomical research. From 1975 to 1995, the KAO rewrote astronomy textbooks. Equipped with a 36-inch reflecting telescope, scientists aboard the KAO discovered rings around Uranus and made interstellar observations regarding the birth of stars and the infrared signature of far-off galaxies. The findings provided an important boost for deep space observation and served as an important predecessor to the Hubble Space Telescope.

On the other side of the stratosphere from the KAO, another unique research lab was created out of seemingly incompatible parts. On July 17, 1975, an Apollo spacecraft launched and docked in space with the Soviet Soyuz spacecraft in a highly publicized moment of peace between Cold War adversaries, a grand gesture of cooperation both scientific and symbolic. Astronauts and cosmonauts worked in tandem for two days before parting ways. After this brief smoothing of Cold War friction, no manned U.S. spaceflights took place for the following six years. NASA and its contractors were instead hard at work developing a reusable spacecraft that could transport and deploy satellites into space, service satellites in orbit and return to Earth — a feat never before attempted. The first orbiter, dubbed *Enterprise*, was unveiled in 1976 and subjected to numerous altitude and landing tests similar to those of the X-24A. Made up of nearly 500,000 parts, Martin Marietta's external fuel tank would become the largest component of the complete, spaceflight-qualified shuttle system. But the silo-sized tank — originally white, but later left its natural orange to save weight — was also a remarkable work of design simplicity.

Martin Marietta's design for Project Viking, however, was entirely different.

Constructed to be the first vehicle to land on Mars, the Viking was referred to by the Los Angeles Times as "a triumph of function over form … perhaps as bizarre as any Martian machine ever conceived by a science fiction writer. If the Viking had wheels instead of footpads, it would resemble the overloaded car of some dust bowl family of the 1930s headed west."[8]

A 28-foot-diameter liquid-oxygen tank, an interior structure of the space shuttle's giant external tank, is cleaned with solvent following pressurization tests, 1984.

Telescopes had enabled people on Earth to lay eyes on Mars as early as the 17th century, but Mariner 4 — launched in 1965 on a General Dynamics Atlas and Lockheed Agena D rocket — provided the first close-up images of the Red Planet. In 1971, Mariner 9 became the first spacecraft to orbit Mars, sending back images of craters, mountains, polar deposits and extinct volcanoes. The logical next step in planetary exploration was to land on the planet's surface.

Martin Marietta designed and built two Mars landers — Viking I and Viking II — and the Titan III with the Centaur upper stages that were needed to launch the Viking landers from Earth.

On July 20, 1976, the seventh anniversary of the first moon landing, the Viking lander separated from its orbiter and plunged toward the surface of Mars. It took

While Mars became fertile ground for exploration, Martin's Titan III rockets also launched the Voyager deep space probes in 1977, headed for Saturn, Jupiter and eventually beyond the edge of the solar system. Voyager carried with it a golden record encoded with audio and visual information about Earth and its life, its people, its music, its landscape and its promise — should it ever be encountered by extraterrestrial intelligence capable of decoding such an artifact.

The external tank for the space shuttle is 154 feet long and 28 feet in diameter, and holds 520,000 gallons of propellant.

The Viking landers weighed 1,300 pounds and were covered in tanks, antennas and funnels. The scientific equipment on the landers included cameras, nuclear power generators, and on-board biology and chemistry labs. Among other objectives, Viking's mission was to gather and test the soil of another world.

19 minutes for engineers on Earth to find out whether their spacecraft had landed safely. The lag between action and information from telemetry data was excruciating. NASA and Martin Marietta engineers at the Jet Propulsion Laboratory in Pasadena, Calif., finally received confirmation that the lander had successfully touched down only 17 seconds later than expected. "Not bad when you're dealing with an automated spacecraft across 225 million miles," said George Sands.[9]

Newspapers and magazines around the world soon published the first pictures taken from the surface of Mars. Less than two months later, on September 3, 1976, the Viking II lander descended safely onto the Martian surface on the opposite side of the planet, beginning a new era of Mars exploration as the two craft continued to gather imagery, sample soil and collect other vital data. Project Viking discovered evidence of dry river valleys and past rainfall — signaling the possibility of life.

A wave of scientific data met with a resurgence of popular interest in space exploration. On April 12, 1981, the space shuttle Columbia launched from the Kennedy Space Center in Cape Canaveral, Fla., on its first mission, beginning an era of manned spaceflight unlike any before or since. Supported by Martin Marietta's sleek external tank weighing nearly 76,000 pounds, Columbia looked more like a sophisticated space plane than the capsulelike design of the Apollo or Viking landers. But the future of space was no longer about races to the moon or style over substance. The goal was sustained human and scientific exploration and discovery.

The Hubble program moved forward with an array of contractors contributing to the effort. Lockheed Missiles and Space Company was selected to build Hubble's Support Systems Module — the spacecraft structure that encloses the Optical Telescope Assembly and the science instruments. Astrophysicist Eric J. Chaisson eloquently explained the revolutionary project:

> Hubble's vaunted technology will not likely produce a new can opener or better washing machine. Nor should it. This giant eye in the sky was built neither to improve our economy nor to challenge our Cold War enemies. Rather, the Hubble Space Telescope is an expression of technological poetry, pure and simple. This magnificent orbiting observatory seeks knowledge for the sake of knowing, discovery for the sake of discovering, to understand cosmic beauty for its own sake. All things considered, the Hubble project is a measure of the extent to which humane beings — human with an "e" — are willing to devote some time, money, and resources to allow our species the opportunity to rise above the mundane activities on planet Earth.[10]

IRAN, IRAQ AND AFGHANISTAN

While international manned spaceflight programs evolved, the Cold War remained rooted in old patterns. Violent and inconclusive proxy wars continued to take the place of nuclear engagement between the two superpowers. Beginning in 1980, the United States and Soviets engaged in an extended period of tense on-again, off-again negotiations regarding nuclear arms control. In 1983, these talks reached a turning point as the world glimpsed a possibility of nuclear war unmatched since the Cuban Missile Crisis.

"NEVER, PERHAPS, IN THE POSTWAR DECADES WAS THE SITUATION IN THE WORLD AS EXPLOSIVE AND HENCE, MORE DIFFICULT AND UNFAVORABLE, AS IN THE FIRST HALF OF THE 1980s."[11]

—SOVIET GENERAL SECRETARY MIKHAIL GORBACHEV, FEBRUARY 1986

President Reagan and Soviet General Secretary Mikhail Gorbachev signing the INF Treaty in the East Room of the White House, Dec. 8, 1987.

ABLE ARCHER

Since 1976, the most dangerous weapon in the Eastern Hemisphere had been the Soviet Strategic Rocket Forces' SS-20 Saber missile system. At 54 feet long and more than 77,000 pounds, the SS-20 had been deployed at nearly 50 installations across the Soviet Union, putting it in range of both Western Europe and East Asia. The SS-20 carried three thermonuclear warheads with an overall blast radius capable of decimating a land area the size of Manhattan. For seven years, the Soviets had the clear upper hand.

Then, in 1983, Martin Marietta's new MGM-31 Pershing II missiles arrived in West Germany. The Pershing system was smaller than the Saber — a little more than half its size and only a fifth of its weight — but far more mobile. With a range of more than 1,000 miles, it could reach the western Soviet Union, and its power and accuracy made the Pershing II capable of destroying hard targets, such as missile silos and command bunkers.

The most impressive feature of the new Pershing was its speed. Upon launch, Martin Marietta's new missile system could reach Soviet targets in only four to six minutes. Suddenly, the United States had not only achieved parity in this high-stakes game of nuclear poker, it also held the trump card: unmatched first-strike capability.

The United States' plan was to negotiate with the Soviets from a position of strength, but by March 1983, the Soviets saw U.S. actions as more than a bluff. They began preparing for a U.S. attack. During a NATO exercise code-named Able Archer 83, the Soviets mistakenly believed the United States was about to actually launch. Brinksmanship had a sobering effect on both superpowers. They went back to the negotiation table, and this time, they were ready to sign one of the most sweeping nuclear treaties in history.

The Intermediate-Range Nuclear Forces Treaty, signed in December 1987 by the United States and the Soviet Union, was the first to effectively eliminate an entire class of nuclear weapons, with the Pershing II and the Soviet SS-20 missiles considered the most threatening. Once again, achieving parity in nuclear deterrents had, in effect, engendered a peaceful Cold War stalemate.

HIT A BULLET WITH A BULLET

U.S. Army officials staring at their radar screens on June 10, 1984, watched in breathless anticipation as two American missiles — one launched from Vandenberg Air Force Base in California, the other from a missile range in the Marshall Islands — hurtled toward each other over the Pacific Ocean.

Lockheed's Homing Overlay Experiment was an opportunity to see if one missile could intercept another in the upper atmosphere. The odds of its success seemed thin at best. As one Army official put it, it was like trying to hit a bullet with a bullet.

The stakes for success could not have been higher. A year earlier, President Ronald Reagan had announced his Strategic Defense Initiative, an ambitious effort to create a defensive "shield" against Soviet missile strikes. The HOE was a key part of the plan, which sought to use a mix of space- and ground-based defensive weapons to protect the U.S. mainland.

The missile that deployed from the Marshall Islands was different from previous missile technologies, which relied on the detonation of a nuclear warhead to destroy everything within a given blast radius. Lockheed's HOE missile was free of nuclear materials, and equipped with its own guidance system and a unique fan that unfurled before contact, increasing the chance of a successful hit.

Moving forward, Lockheed would use its revolutionary hit-to-kill technology to intercept missiles further away and higher from their intended targets using its Terminal High Altitude Area Defense. Transferred from the ground to the sea, the hit-to-kill technology is at the heart of Lockheed's Aegis ballistic missile defense, which played a key role in the creation of a multilayered defense shield over Europe, bringing the project full circle in less than three decades.

As the dummy ICBM streaked from Vandenberg Air Force Base toward its target at 20,000 miles per hour, Lockheed's hit-to-kill vehicle locked into position and promptly unfurled its ribbed metal plate. When the two missiles met at an altitude of about 90,000 feet, the sheer force of the impact destroyed both missiles. The world's first successful non-nuclear defensive missile had arrived.

After Lockheed and Martin Marietta merged in the mid-1990s, Lockheed's HOE technology was combined with Martin Marietta's Patriot missile defense system to create the PAC-3, capable of destroying incoming tactical ballistic missiles, cruise missiles and aircraft without the use of an explosive warhead.

STABILIZING IN SPACE

During this time, manned spaceflight experienced a renaissance. The first nine space shuttle launches had met with resounding success and public approval. Astronauts tested extravehicular tools like a robotic arm capable of docking with satellites and other spacecraft. With more spacewalks and extravehicular work to be done in space, the need for precision motion control became critical.

To meet this need, Martin Marietta designed and built the Manned Maneuvering Unit, a "jetpack" that allowed astronauts to control their movements in space without being tethered to the shuttle. With 24 hand-controlled thrusters, the backpack gave the astronauts subtle navigation and speed control. After the first test flights in space in early 1984, the MMU was employed in its first satellite retrieval mission on April 11.

Astronaut Bruce McCandless flies 180 miles above the coast of southwest Africa on the first space mission of the Manned Maneuvering Unit, 1984.

Back on Earth, Lockheed technicians had finally finished building and integrating NASA's Hubble Space Telescope and prepared it for launch. When Princeton astrophysicist Lyman Spitzer theorized in 1946 about positioning a large telescope in space, developing such technology was still out of reach. Decades later, retrieving imagery from millions of light years away was almost a reality. The primary goals of Hubble were to establish the expansion speed and age of the universe, examine ultraviolet emissions of quasars, and inaugurate an unprecedented golden age of astronomy.

Before Hubble would be launched, however, tragedy struck. On January 28, 1986, the shuttle Challenger exploded 73 seconds after liftoff, killing all seven crew members aboard, including the first civilian shuttle passenger, schoolteacher Christa McAuliffe. The televised disaster shocked America and the world and grounded the U.S. space program's shuttle fleet for nearly three years.

SEEING FARTHER

After an extensive investigation of what went wrong in the Challenger tragedy, new flight processes and hardware configuration were developed to prevent the problem in the future. Shuttle launches resumed in September 1988, and NASA prepared Hubble for a new launch date.

Meanwhile, on May 4, 1989, another deep space robotic probe made headlines. Borrowing spare parts from previous missions such as Voyager and Mariner 9, Martin Marietta created the Magellan spacecraft to map the surface of Venus using Synthetic Aperture Radar. SAR technology developed by Lockheed Martin heritage company Goodyear Aircraft Company (later renamed Goodyear Aerospace) had been put to use in the nonmilitary arena beginning in the 1970s. It proved especially useful in mapping equatorial regions of Earth and other areas often shrouded in clouds. Its use on Magellan marked the first attempt to use SAR for interplanetary mapping.

Magellan reached Venus and settled into orbit on August 10, 1990, but problems soon surfaced and communication faltered. "Radar operations had to be postponed, as engineers began the frustrating task of trying to diagnose and treat an ailing spacecraft 155 million miles beyond their reach," The New York Times reported.[12]

Following the first orbital mission of the Columbia space shuttle in April 1981, Columbia launched three more times between November 1981 and June 1982. In 1983, a second shuttle, Challenger, sent the first U.S. woman and first African American astronauts into space — Sally Ride and Guion Bluford.

Advances in SAR processing algorithms have provided image quality that greatly enhances target detection and identification, 1990s.

As was the case with Martin Marietta's earlier Viking crafts, redundant systems and fault-tolerance instructions allowed engineers to restore communication. Magellan remained in orbit until 1994, producing detailed radar maps and images of geologic formations never seen before.

SEEING CLEARLY

While Magellan engineers were able to quickly avoid a potential mission failure, the Hubble Space Telescope was not as fortunate. Hubble was lofted into space by the shuttle Discovery on April 24, 1990, released into orbit the following day and set to gaze deeper into space than any telescope in history.

Despite the precautions taken by Lockheed in its revolutionary Sunnyvale clean room, the deep space images captured by the telescope came back blurry. The flaw on the edge of Hubble's primary mirror was later found to be off by 1/50 the width of a human hair — wide enough to mar Hubble's images.

The planned servicing missions of Hubble showcased the value and foresight of building a manned space shuttle program capable of servicing satellites in orbit. Supported by Lockheed, the first Hubble servicing mission launched on December 2, 1993. The space shuttle carried a more advanced Wide Field Camera and a corrective optics device intended to cure Hubble's chromatic aberration and poised the U.S. manned spaceflight program for a whole new era of combined human and robotic capabilities in space.

The dramatic servicing mission united the talents of thousands of aerospace engineers and technicians, and integrated dozens of advances pioneered by Lockheed, Martin Marietta and their heritage companies. Riding on the back of the external fuel tank, the shuttle reached orbit and successfully docked with Hubble.

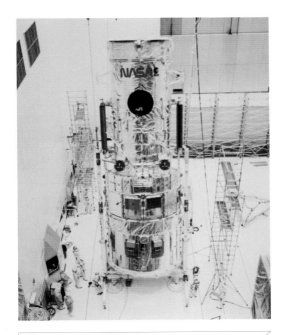

The Hubble Space Telescope is prepared for launch.

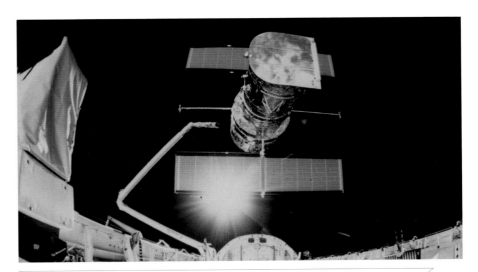

The Hubble Space Telescope was deployed into a 380-mile orbit by the STS-31 crew of the space shuttle Discovery. Photographed just after being released from the Remote Manipulator System robot arm, April 25, 1990.

The volcanic surface of Venus as compiled from satellite images taken by the Magellan spacecraft, 1993.

Martin Marietta's Magellan spacecraft, designed to radar-map Venus, is prepared for final testing before delivery to Kennedy Space Center, 1988.

For five days, astronauts carefully replaced and installed the telescope's corrective "eyeglasses" and returned home safely, landing at Kennedy Space Center on December 13. Soon, the telescope was recording not only spectacular visions from within our solar system but also the clearest view of Pluto that astronomers had ever seen. Scientists could peer into the farthest known reaches of space and time, and the sights were astounding.

TENSIONS MELT

After Reagan and Gorbachev signed the Intermediate-Range Nuclear Forces Treaty in December 1987, a series of reforms by Gorbachev attempted to move the Soviet system toward an increasingly democratic foundation. The communist-bloc Eastern European countries that once formed the Iron Curtain began to fall in 1989 and 1990, paving the way for democracy in Poland, Hungary, Czechoslovakia and East Germany. The strip of concrete and barbed wire separating East and West Berlin still stood. East German and Soviet expatriates launched a westward exodus, streaming across borders into democratic lands. Public demonstrators poured into East and West Berlin, echoing Reagan's impassioned 1987 challenge for Gorbachev to "tear down this wall!"

On November 9, 1989, the Berlin Wall began to fall. The official unification of Germany was formalized on July 1, 1990. By the following year, the Soviet Union had disintegrated, leading to the birth of 15 independent and largely democratic republics. The Cold War was over.

Astronauts F. Story Musgrave (top) and Jeffrey A. Hoffman, orbiting the Earth at an altitude of 325 miles, wrap up the final of five spacewalks to service the Hubble Space Telescope, 1993.

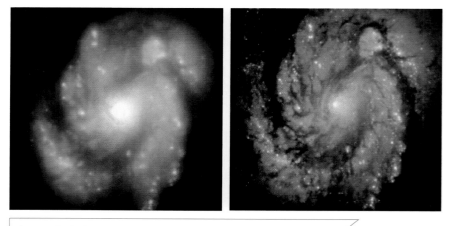

Images taken before and after the first Hubble servicing mission, which installed corrective optics. The mission helped the space telescope realize its potential and also validated the in-orbit repair capabilities engendered by the space shuttle program, 1993.

The end of the Iraq-Iran War in 1988 and the withdrawal of Soviet troops from Afghanistan in 1989 might have foretold an easing of Middle Eastern tensions, as well, but such quick peace was not to be. On August 2, 1990, Iraq invaded Kuwait, achieving a fast and decisive victory condemned by the United Nations and nearly all world powers. The Cold War had ended, but Saddam Hussein's refusal to withdraw from Kuwait set the stage for a global military engagement in the Middle East.

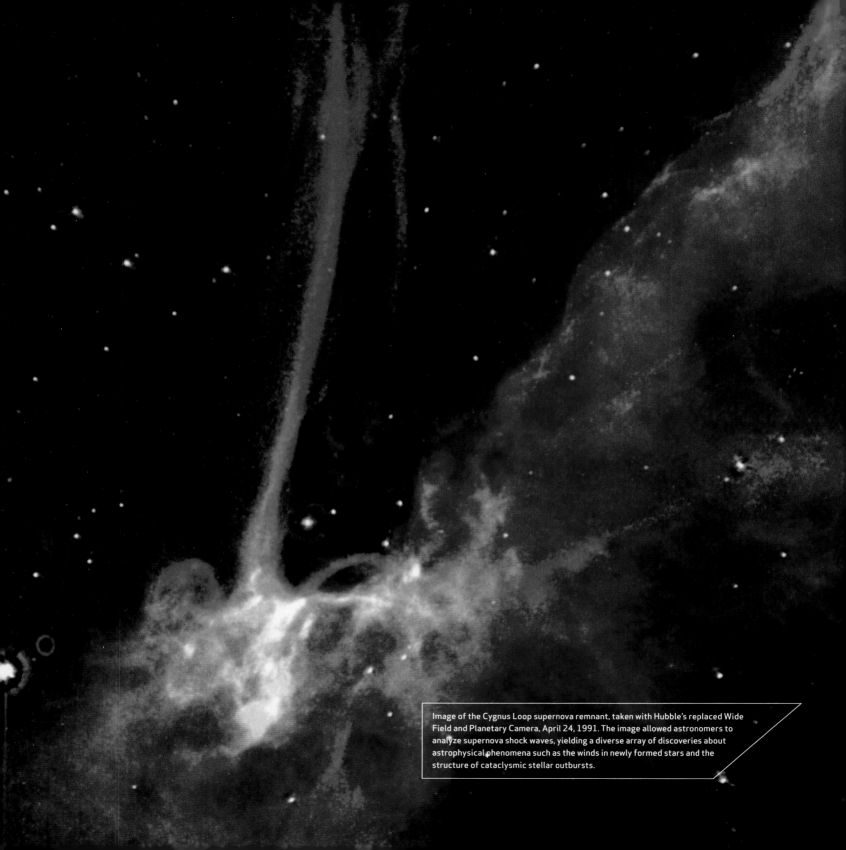

Image of the Cygnus Loop supernova remnant, taken with Hubble's replaced Wide Field and Planetary Camera, April 24, 1991. The image allowed astronomers to analyze supernova shock waves, yielding a diverse array of discoveries about astrophysical phenomena such as the winds in newly formed stars and the structure of cataclysmic stellar outbursts.

CHAPTER 7

SILICON AND SCREENS

The Digital Age Accelerates
1991–2001

"THE GULF WAR WAS THE CATALYST. … THE GPS WAS TOTALLY OPERATIONAL BY THAT TIME. THE IMAGING SATELLITES WERE TOTALLY OPERATIONAL. THE INTERNET HAD MATURED ENOUGH. … IT WAS A VERY, VERY DIFFERENT WORLD."[1]

—SAM ARAKI

SIDE BY SIDE

On the left-hand monitor, analysts scrutinized a satellite image of the Iraq desert in full color. On the right, they zoomed in, rotated and enhanced the overhead view in high-resolution black-and-white, gleaning more detail with only a few keystrokes. By today's standards, the twin-monitor Lockheed IDEX II Workstation is an unwieldy relic. But in 1991, it was nothing short of revolutionary.

From 1991 to 2003, the Lockheed Imagery Data Exploitation (IDEX II) Workstation analyzed digital reconnaissance imagery. This intelligence could now be retrieved, stored, analyzed and dissemminated at unprecedented speeds. [Inset] An F-16 Low Altitude Navigation and Targeting Infrared for Night (LANTIRN) system allowed for low-altitude night flights, 1985.

Martin Marietta LANTIRN pod mounted on an F-16 Fighting Falcon, 1990s.

Cold War image analysts once hunched over light boards, magnifying tools in hand, struggling to decipher the intelligence hidden in photographic film. By the time images were pieced together, de-warped and analyzed, enemy targets might have changed position, hot leads turned cold. With the Imagery Data Exploitation program, Lockheed's engineers traded film for pixels, hoping to harness silicon semiconductors to supercharge the global intelligence community. They succeeded.

Soon, analysts could annotate images of Iraqi airfield activity and troop movement, quickly relaying the intel to military commanders. And as Lockheed's IDEX system employed computer technology to see enemy movement more clearly, Martin Marietta found a way to see in the dark.

Zoom in. Track eastward. Enhance.

Mounted under the left side of an F-16, the AN/AAQ-13 navigation pod's radar allowed the test pilot to maintain a preset altitude of as low as 100 feet, automatically avoiding shifts in terrain while superimposing a grainy image of the battlefield on the head-up display. Mounted under the right side of the fuselage, the AN/AAQ-14 targeting pod's infrared and laser rangefinder could track and deliver precision ordnance to moving targets. First conceived in 1981 and ready for its first combat deployment in the Middle East theater, Martin Marietta's high-tech LANTIRN system, short for Low Altitude Navigation and Targeting Infrared for Night, had given pilots the ability to automatically fly and fight over any terrain, in any weather, day or night. The world's first around-the-clock aerial strike force had been born.

In the opening hours of Operation Desert Storm, technology took a forward position on the battlefield. Stealth technology, precision-guided munitions and electronic warfare prepared coalition forces to engage Saddam Hussein's Iraqi forces, the world's fourth-largest army at the time, from a position of overwhelming strength. Digital and information technology would prove pivotal in the war and would soon assume a similarly central role in postwar military and civilian circles. Throughout the 1990s, technology transformed the global battlefield and unlocked more mysteries of space. Amid the challenges of terrorist threats and expanded access to information, the aerospace industry adapted with a series of mergers that ultimately united two of its pioneers into a single leader: Lockheed Martin Corporation.

WATCHING DESERT SHIELD

By 1990, the computer age had arrived. Military and intelligence communities had used computer systems in the past, but with the advent of Apple's graphic user interface in 1984 and the Microsoft Windows GUI system in 1990, personal computers began to take up residence in ordinary homes and offices nationwide. Americans had more than 54 million computers up and running by the start of the decade, and the World Wide Web established a foundation for the coming information age.

As faster microprocessors spurred image analysts, military commanders and fighter pilots to rely on the data that appeared on their computer screens, live television brought the urgency of the Persian Gulf conflict to American living rooms. Kuwait City

U.S. soldiers and vehicles arrive in Saudi Arabia aboard a Lockheed C-5 Galaxy as part of Operation Desert Shield. Coverage by NBC, ABC, CBS and especially CNN became part and parcel of the high-tech war, 1990.

woke up to the sounds of Saddam Hussein's 100,000 troops and tanks on August 2, 1990, and Saddam swiftly annexed the territory. Televised images of the attack and occupation reached a global audience. Iraqi forces soon threatened the border of Saudi Arabia as well.

As President George H. W. Bush famously promised on August 5, "This will not stand."[2] Crews in Lockheed land-based P-3 Orion and carrier-based S-3 Viking patrol aircraft were the first Allied aircraft on the scene, and they provided key surveillance, identification and interdiction of surface shipping over the first few crucial days of the Iraqi occupation. But beyond these small patrol squadrons, the United States had no significant air forces in the Middle East.

With Saudi King Fahd's approval, Bush ordered a massive mobilization effort, known as Operation Desert Shield. Soon, hundreds of Lockheed C-141s, C-5s and C-130s landed at Dhahran Air Base. In just 22 days, Desert Shield airlifts surpassed the tonnage delivered during the entire 11 months of the Berlin Blockade in 1948 and 1949. As the United States mobilized for war, projects like Lockheed's F-117 Nighthawk and Martin Marietta's Patriot missile system prepared to enter combat.

When Desert Shield became Desert Storm, S-3 Vikings entered active combat duty, supporting sorties with aerial refueling and attacking enemy air defenses such as a Silkworm missile launch site and Saddam Hussein's ocean-going yacht.

Patriot missiles were modified with an advanced propulsion system that increased the missile's operating range and speed. Technicians inspect wiring on Patriot air-defense missile sections before final assembly, 1990.

DEFENSE VS. OFFENSE

On Aug. 5, 1990, just three days after Saddam Hussein's invasion of Kuwait, Richard Howell, the director of Martin Marietta's Patriot program, received a phone call informing him that the time for deployment had finally come. In 1968, Martin Marietta had won a contract to develop a mobile system of large missile canisters loaded onto the backs of truck transports, capable of firing highly maneuverable intercepts that could keep pace with nimble Soviet jets. After a complex design, development and testing phase, the Patriot — Phased Array Track Intercept of Target — missile defense system was needed in the Middle East.

The challenge? The Patriot system required Martin Marietta's PAC-2 missiles, and only three of these existed. Working with Raytheon Company's Missile Systems Division, subcontractor Martin Marietta ramped up production of the PAC-2s as well

Martin Marietta built missiles, canisters and launch stations for Patriot, the nation's most advanced surface-to-air defense missile, which scored six intercepts in as many firings during its final development tests, 1981.

as the Patriot's missile containers and launcher vehicles, working around the clock in 12-hour shifts. By January 1991, the Orlando facility had readied more than 400 missiles for combat.

In the intervening months, regional powers such as Saudi Arabia, Egypt and Syria had joined the United States, the United Kingdom, France and nearly 50 other nations in condemning Saddam's actions. After many attempts at peaceful diplomacy, the United Nations issued a deadline for his withdrawal. When the January 15 date came and went and Saddam remained in Kuwait, war became imminent. Two days later, Desert Shield became Desert Storm.

THE FIRST NIGHT

At 3 a.m. on Jan. 17, 1991, crews in more than 600 aircraft and helicopters launched a coordinated aerial campaign against Iraqi forces. Eight Apache helicopter pilots started the action, destroying Iraqi early warning radar sites with Martin Marietta AGM-114 Hellfire laser- and radar-guided munitions. British aircraft then aimed for Saddam's runways, while pilots flying in Lockheed's F-117 Nighthawk, the first stealth aircraft to see combat, headed directly for the Iraqi capital. The Nighthawk accounted for about 5 percent of this initial air offensive. But its role in the opening hours of the war was absolutely crucial.

"We sort of believed in stealth technology, but we hadn't really proven it at the time," said pilot Lt. Col. Joseph Salata Jr. "There was probably just a little bit of nervousness there ... until we saw what happened on the first night. We saw how successful we really could be. We saw that the Skunk Works really did design a great stealth airplane."[3]

Under cover of night, the 37th Tactical Fighter Wing flew 10 of its black jets directly into Baghdad, slipping in unseen by enemy radar. The first targets: Iraq's integrated operations centers, air defense control headquarters, its main telecommunications tower and even Saddam's palace grounds. The first F-117 that dropped its laser-guided ordnance scored a direct hit on the ventilation shaft of the telecommunications building, a strike so accurate it conjured cinematic comparisons to Luke Skywalker's bull's-eye shot into the exhaust port of the Death Star. Infrared video captured by the F-117's bomb-bay cameras was replayed repeatedly on CNN.

With precision munitions, F-117s scored 13 similar hits in 17 attempts. More waves followed. Throughout that first night, the stealth fighter-bombers laid waste to 37 strategic targets across the Iraqi capital, severing the central nervous system of Iraq's Integrated Air Defenses and paving the way for conventional aircraft to enter the fight. Despite a blind barrage of enemy anti-aircraft artillery, not one F-117 was lost: When enemies can't see a target, they can't hit it.

Making up only 2 to 3 percent of coalition forces, the stealth F-117 Nighthawk accounted for about 35 percent of first-night targets and overall hit rates of 75 percent.

The Lockheed-built F-117 officially took its place as the world's first invisible aircraft.

The *USS Leyte Gulf* Aegis-class guided missile cruiser saw service in Operation Desert Storm.

F-117s were relocated from Groom Lake, Nev., to the Tonapah Test Range in 1983. The aircraft were only flown at night to preserve the project's secrecy.

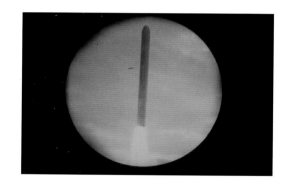

Nearly 300 Tomahawks were fired during the war using Martin Marietta's MK-41 Vertical Launching System. In January 1993, cruise missiles fired against Iraqi targets were launched using this VLS system. This photo of a Tomahawk missile fired from an SSN-688 Attack Class submarine was taken through a periscope during Desert Storm, 1991.

The Nighthawk was not the only weapon that employed low-observability technology and precision guidance. Also proving highly effective in the war's first night was the Tomahawk cruise missile, developed by General Dynamics in the 1970s and using Martin Marietta's MK-41 Vertical Launching System on Aegis-class cruisers and destroyers. Minutes after the initial F-117 strikes, the first Tomahawk Land Attack Missile fired in combat history was launched from the USS *San Jacinto* in the Red Sea. Its target was preprogrammed, but its flightpath could shift on a dime. Over water, the missile was guided by a system of gyroscopes and sensors that allowed it to change speed and direction. Once it reached land, the more precise TERCOM took over, evading radar while rocketing at speeds of 550 miles per hour only 100 to 200 feet off the ground.

More than 100 Tomahawks were fired in the first night alone, with about 94 percent reaching their targets and providing cover for other coalition aircraft.

Key to Hellfire's accuracy was another Martin Marietta system on the nose of the Apache: TADS/PNVS (Target Acquisition Designation Sight/Pilot Night Vision System) that enabled day or night attack.

In a single night, the air attack disabled the Iraqi forces completely. Moreover, the advent of electronic warfare and guided munitions marked a great departure from the days of carpet bombing. This was precision warfare.

THE MORNING AFTER

Within 24 hours of the first airstrikes, it became clear that the Gulf War could be won quickly. Unable to take down the Nighthawks, the Iraqi force was soon radar-blind and nearly powerless against the coalition's full aerial assault. Meanwhile, Tomahawk missiles continued to rain down, using Martin Marietta's MK-41 Vertical Launching System, developed in 1986, which turned the sea-based Aegis Combat System into a formidable first-strike weapon. The system's versatility was proved when the Aegis-equipped cruiser USS *Bunker Hill* took over tactical control of 26 warships and more than 300 aircraft, directing attacks against Iraqi forces and coordinating the interception of enemy missiles.

These enemy missiles, known as Scuds, emerged in the war's first week as a formidable threat to coalition forces and neighboring countries. Hoping to divert attention from the ongoing aerial attack, Iraqi Scud missiles targeted Israel and Saudi Arabia. Live television audiences and U.S. soldiers watched night-vision footage of PAC-2 missiles, gleaming like green lasers in the night sky, protecting allied positions from Tel Aviv to Riyadh.

While Patriot missiles intercepted the majority of Iraqi Scuds, three slipped through the defensive system and struck Israel on January 19, injuring about 17 people. Bush rushed Patriots into Israel while persuading the country not to retaliate. Israel agreed to stay on the sidelines while preparing to ward off future attacks.

High-tech defensive measures like the Patriot had to work in tandem with equally advanced offensive capabilities, though. Throughout the first night and the next morning, F-15s and F-16s, equipped with Martin Marietta's LANTIRN pods, went directly after Scud launchers and support sites. Less than 18 hours after the first

The Hellfire missile system seeker homes in on a laser-illuminated target in the laboratory. The Hellfire is an air-launched antiarmor missile, the primary armament for the Army AH-64 Apache.

"THANK GOD THAT WHEN THOSE SCUDS CAME IN, THE PEOPLE OF SAUDI ARABIA AND ISRAEL AND THE BRAVE FORCES OF OUR COALITION HAD MORE TO PROTECT THEIR LIVES THAN SOME ABSTRACT THEORY OF DETERRENCE. THANK GOD FOR THE PATRIOT MISSILE."[4]

—PRESIDENT GEORGE H. W. BUSH, 1991

Though the F-16 proved most valuable as a fighter-bomber during the Gulf War, a Fighting Falcon also shot down a key Iraq Mig-25 during a dogfight in the months that followed the campaign. The dark gray pods under the engine intake are LANTIRN navigation and targeting systems, 1991.

strike on Baghdad, however, the Middle East winter reared its head, with thunderstorms, thick cloud cover and dense fog creating havoc for air sorties. Military DMSP weather satellites, launched before the war on Atlas rockets, provided support during this eight-day environmental challenge. Coalition forces were still able to destroy Iraqi nuclear, chemical and biological sites.

When the weather broke, the Allied air campaign continued its all-out assault on the Iraqi Integrated Air Defenses, which included surface-to-air and anti-aircraft missiles, radar, fighter aircraft, and command and control centers. Though intended as a dogfighter, the multirole F-16 showed its versatility in Desert Storm and was mainly used as a fighter-bomber. Some 249 Fighting Falcons contributed to the war effort, taking out airfields, military production facilities and missile sites. In fact, more missions were flown by the F-16s than by any other aircraft. But the stealth aircraft created by Skunk Works served as the linchpin of the coalition's strategic air campaign from start to finish. Continuing its stellar combat run, the F-117 Nighthawk flew less than 3 percent of Desert Storm's total attack sorties but destroyed nearly 40 percent of the strategic targets. Its accuracy and mission success rate was simply astounding.

A former Secretary of the Air Force put the accomplishments in perspective: "In World War II it could take 9,000 bombs to hit a target the size of an aircraft shelter. In Vietnam, 300. Today [May 1991] we can do it with one laser-guided munition from an F-117."[5]

The Patriot system, seen here intercepting Scud missiles over Tel Aviv, immediately came to symbolize the futuristic war drama in the Middle East. It also marked the first combat exchange between ballistic and defensive missiles in history, and the beginnings of today's multilayered air missile defense shield.

EVOLVING ARTILLERY

MLRS: THE STORM BRINGER

On an arid patch of land where the borders of Iraq, Saudi Arabia and Kuwait meet, 10 armored vehicles gathered on Feb. 13, 1991, and took up positions along a two-mile stretch of desert. These mobile rocket launchers, dubbed the Multiple Launch Rocket System, were the newest weapons in the U.S. Army's arsenal, sophisticated artillery guns designed to fire more warheads faster and farther than any of their predecessors.

Their mission was to strike enemy defensive positions from a distance at a furious pace, effectively fragmenting the Iraqi army, which could then be engaged by U.S. ground forces. The U.S. troops were ready. The MLRS, however, was untested. But when the "go" sign was given that evening, signaling the first official combat launch of an MLRS, all doubts were instantly vanquished.

The vehicles, firing in concert as a single unit, launched more than 100 rockets in a single minute, pummeling targets in

southern Iraq with unprecedented fury. In the coming days, relentless attacks from MLRS vehicles would demoralize Iraqi soldiers on the ground, ushering in a quick and decisive victory for U.S. forces.

Propped atop an M2 Bradley Fighting Vehicle chassis, an MLRS allowed a three-man crew to drive to a site, release its missiles and speed off at up to 36 mph across any terrain, in what became known as a "shoot and scoot" strategy. Airlifted via Lockheed C-5 Galaxy transports, it was the ultimate mobile artillery piece, easily moved from battlefield to battlefield as the need arose.

Once unleashed in the Persian Gulf, Iraqi soldiers quickly dubbed the bomblets dropped by MLRS missiles "steel rain." The bomblets' reputation led many Iraqi artillery officers to stay in their bunkers, making it easier for U.S. ground forces to slip in and capture enemy positions.

Jointly developed by the United States, the United Kingdom, Germany and France, the first MLRS model officially entered service in 1983, gradually developing into the mobile missile system used so successfully during Operation Desert Storm. Some 201 MLRS vehicles fired 9,660 M77 rockets, unleashing 6,221,040 bomblets on Iraqi targets.

COPPERHEAD

On the morning of Feb. 7, 1991, a team of artillery commanders gathered in a dusty command post along the Iraq-Kuwait border to lay out the directives for the day. Their primary objective: a line of 40-foot-tall observation towers to the north. Intelligence reports had revealed that the towers were being used to direct the planting of land mines around Allied positions.

The artillery commanders' aim was to take out the towers as quickly and accurately as possible. And they had just the weapon to do it: a new laser-guided artillery round, the first cannon-fired "smart" munition of its kind, called Copperhead.

Just before 3 p.m., a U.S. armored vehicle entered the area and locked on to one of the towers with an invisible laser beam. Satellites in the sky verified its position and relayed the information to a nearby 155 mm howitzer cannon. It fired, releasing a Copperhead that followed the laser straight to its target, pulverizing the tower. Three minutes later, another Copperhead hit its mark, crippling the second tower. The Copperhead, named after the venomous North American snake, had found a new home in the deserts of Iraq.

Before the Copperhead, new cannon munitions offered more power and longer range but rarely greater accuracy. That changed in 1975, when Martin Marietta developed the world's first cannon-launched guided projectile. Once fired, the Copperhead sprouted small wings and control fins and glided along the path of the laser, delivering warheads to targets with unrivaled accuracy.

Copperheads were used to destroy tanks, border posts and strategic facilities throughout Iraq, softening defenses before a given campaign's main offensive.

The U.S. Army's 155 mm laser-guided projectile — known as the Copperhead — is fired from a M198 Howitzer at a target tank.

Lockheed Martin built the ground-control system for the satellite system, which provides precise positional accuracy. New GPS software helped track the new Block IIR GPS satellites shown in an artist's rendering.

GROUND WAR BEGINS AND ENDS

Coalition forces had achieved and maintained air supremacy in the Persian Gulf. Through mid-February 1991, precision weapons destroyed more than 1,000 Iraqi tanks and 300 artillery pieces. Meanwhile, airlifts carried out by C-130s and C-141s transported troops and vehicles into Rafah, Egypt, in preparation for the coming ground attack. Aerial reconnaissance and mature GPS technology assisted in this ground war, another well-choreographed campaign of surgical precision.

On February 23, Iraqi forces finished setting fire to hundreds of oil wells throughout Kuwait. The following day, Bush ordered the commencement of the ground campaign. The attack met with only minimal resistance. Coalition air forces had already destroyed most of the Iraqi ground detail, and remaining Iraqi troops surrendered by the tens of thousands, with reports claiming that one unit even surrendered to a CNN news crew.

The value of a mature GPS was underscored in the opening hours of the Gulf War ground attack, the first time the system was used in combat. Since its development by the Air Force and initial launch for the U.S. Department of Defense in 1978, Global Positioning System satellite navigation had become a helpful tool for military operations. In 1991, with the best aerial reconnaissance analyzed in real time by IDEX workstation operators, ground troops and commanders used GPS to triangulate their exact position in a vast, empty desert bereft of landmarks. Tanks and infantry crews could shift their attack plans in real time, outmaneuvering Iraqi forces as they shifted position up to the moment of engagement.

The technology helped in other basic ways, as well. "GPS was a godsend for ground troops traversing the desert, especially in the frequent sandstorms," wrote Air Force Magazine. "Tank crews and drivers of all sorts of vehicles swore by the system. Meal trucks were equipped with GPS receivers to enable drivers to find and feed soldiers of frontline units widely dispersed among the dunes."[6]

Kuwaiti soldiers guard a roadside checkpoint following the withdrawal of Iraqi forces, March 1991.

All told, the ground campaign lasted about 100 hours, effectively liberating Kuwait and driving Iraqi forces back over their border. On February 26, Saddam Hussein announced the withdrawal of Iraqi occupation forces. The following day, Bush declared a cessation of hostilities and laid out initial terms for the cease-fire, bringing to a close one of the most coordinated and decisive military campaigns in history.

The end of the Cold War and a short-lived peace in the Middle East did create great change throughout the aerospace industry. The impressive televised debut of electronic warfare helped push technology forward in the postwar era, as well, and soon created ripple effects throughout both military and civilian waters.

POSTWAR PEACE?

As the Gulf War had proved, American military might was peerless. There were no superpowers with which to keep pace. International cooperation seemed the new order of the day.

Beginning in October 1991, the Madrid Conference brought together the United States and Soviet Union in hopes of brokering a peace treaty between the Israeli, Palestinian and Arab nations of Syria, Lebanon and Jordan. Incoming U.S. President Bill Clinton helped lead the peace effort. In September 1993, Clinton hosted a public signing ceremony of the Oslo Accords in Washington, D.C., bringing together Israeli Prime Minister Yitzhak Rabin and PLO Chairman Yasser Arafat for their first face-to-face attempt at reconciliation.

Peace became a real possibility, a notion underscored in July 1993 when Defense Secretary William Perry called together executives of the nation's largest defense contractors for a dinner party that Martin Marietta CEO Norm Augustine famously referred to as "The Last Supper." Perry told them the Pentagon's budget would drastically shrink. The message was simple: It was time to streamline and consolidate. Lockheed and Martin Marietta had each independently researched prospective merger candidates after that meeting and unknowingly placed each other at the top of their respective short lists.

The two companies had much in common. Each had a rich heritage, with roots in the earliest days of aviation. Both had adapted to meet the global challenges of each era. And both believed in strengthening their companies for the long term instead of selling off divisions to make a quick profit.

The phone rang shortly after 5 p.m. on March 19, 1994, catching Augustine just as he was about to head home for the evening. Augustine had spent his Saturday at the company's headquarters in Bethesda, Md., conferring with his top lieutenants about the company's bid to acquire rival aircraft manufacturer Grumman Corp. Martin Marietta had offered $1.93 billion, but Grumman wanted more.

Lockheed Martin executives Norman R. Augustine and Daniel M. Tellep at the news conference announcing the completion of the merger of Lockheed and Martin Marietta to form Lockheed Martin Corporation, March 15, 1995.

When he picked up the phone later that evening, however, he found Lockheed CEO Daniel M. Tellep on the line.

"Would you have any interest," Tellep asked Augustine, "in putting Martin Marietta and Lockheed together — a merger of equals?"[7]

Two days later, the top executives of each company gathered for a secret meeting in the Hyatt Regency in Phoenix. Over room service deli platters, they tackled the biggest issue: Could the two company cultures ever become one? The potential merger even warranted its own codenames. Lockheed was known as "Lunar," Martin Marietta as "Mars," and the deal itself as "Earthquake."

IT DRIVES RAPID CHANGE

Lockheed Martin's Display System Replacement interfaces with a host computer system to replace end-of-life display generation equipment and gives air traffic controllers modern replacements for aging plan view displays, computer readout displays, and flight data input/output devices, 1995.

AIR TRAFFIC CONTROL

Beginning in the mid-1980s, the FAA took steps to modernize its systems. In 1985, IBM Federal Systems, which would later be acquired by Lockheed Martin, began installing the Host Computer System, which provided more than five times the capacity of the previous generation of FAA computer processors. The system was also 10 times faster and more reliable and easier to maintain. Martin Marietta also participated in this effort, overhauling and integrating the air traffic control system. Beginning in 1983, the company worked with the FAA to manage and integrate new and upgraded systems to ensure they worked as a unified entity. By the mid-1990s, a merged Lockheed Martin Air Traffic Management developed the Display System Replacement project, which upgraded the FAA's 30-year-old equipment with state-of-the-art displays and software for air traffic controllers.

3D GRAPHICS

Following its success with the IDEX system, Lockheed elevated its expertise in computer chip design and manufacturing to a new level in 1996. Forming an agreement with processor powerhouse Intel, Lockheed Martin looked to develop a 3D graphic accelerator chip for use in high-end and consumer computer systems alike. Complex computer images were notoriously large files, which required a secondary and specialized electronic circuit to quickly process the advanced mathematics of graphics and video. In a growing field of graphics-heavy computer applications, the 3D chip set was poised to take the world by storm. The chip was expected to offer "five to 10 times the performance of currently available graphics solutions," according to Gary P. Mann, president of Lockheed Martin Commercial Systems Group.[8]

Lockheed Martin simulation software and hardware, originally developed for defense applications, is tested for use in the entertainment industry, 1993.

WEATHER RADAR

In 1996, Lockheed Martin expanded its commitment to global weather analysis with the NEXRAD (Next-Generation Radar) WSR-98D Doppler Weather radar system. Formed through a joint venture with the China Meteorological Administration, the advanced weather system could forecast a wide range of meteorological events, providing vital early warning data used to conserve natural resources and, hopefully, save lives. This weather radar infrastructure was ultimately adopted nationwide, with a network of more than 150 locations predicting severe storms throughout the continental United States, as well as Hawaii and Alaska. Developing nations such as Romania have adopted the technology, as well.

The first Titan IV/Centaur was launched successfully from Cape Canaveral Air Force Station in early February 1994, to place the Milstar communications satellite into orbit.

The NEXRAD advanced Doppler weather radar displays radar data on the Principal User Processor. The PUP allows operators to access more than 70 weather products quickly and easily by using the graphic selection tablet, mouse or keyboard. About 160 of the radars are being installed throughout the United States and at selected international locations for the National Weather Service, the Department of Transportation (FAA) and the Department of Defense.

COMMUNICATIONS

Though Lockheed Martin's focus on weapons systems was re-evaluated in the post-Gulf War era, its satellite and communications technology continued to support all branches of the armed services as well as commercial customers. The first in a constellation of military communications satellites known as Milstar (short for Military Strategic and Tactical Relay) was sent into orbit by a next-generation Titan IV launch vehicle in February 1994. A second satellite followed in November 1995. A total of 5 Milstar spacecraft were ultimately launched, providing consistent jam-resistant communications infrastructure for the U.S. Army, Navy, Air Force, Marines and Coast Guard.

The Lockheed Martin star logo is drawn from both predecessor companies. During World War I, the Glenn L. Martin Company adopted a logo very similar to the star-in-a-circle design used by the U.S. Army Air Corps, and Allan Lockheed designed a star logo when Lockheed introduced the Vega in the 1920s.

The way Tellep saw it, the merger was a marriage made in heaven, and the companies treated it as such, with each making sacrifices during negotiations for the greater good of the union. The new company, with a newly designed star logo, would be called Lockheed Martin, only because Martin Lockheed sounded too much like an individual's name. Lockheed executives would move to Martin Marietta's headquarters in Maryland, but everyone would get a new office and a fresh start.

Most importantly, the four sectors of the merged company — aeronautics, electronics, information and technology services, and space and strategic missiles — would be balanced between Lockheed and Martin managers, providing equal leadership opportunities for both sides.

The secrecy held, even during antitrust obstacles and tough decisions about who would hold the top leadership position at the merged company. Only 24 hours before the deal was announced, however, reporters from the nation's top newspapers got wise, and on Aug. 29, 1994, The New York Times ran a story speculating that one of the companies was trying to buy out the other. Augustine set the record straight and came clean that Lockheed and Martin were attempting a merger. The leak was a relief for both sides, and even though the details of the deal still had to be solidified, both sides were committed to the merger and said a thankful farewell to six months of secrecy.

On March 16, 1995, the merger became official, uniting what were then the second- and third-largest American defense contractors.

During the transition period, the synergy between the companies soon became evident. The partnership led to stunning advances in the air, on land, in space and in cyberspace, and paved the way for Lockheed Martin to diversify beyond military contracts and become the largest provider of IT services, systems integration, and training to the U.S. government.

UNDERSTANDING SPACE

The merger between Lockheed and Martin Marietta wasn't the only unification effort in the aerospace industry in the mid-1990s. Lockheed Martin and the companies formed in other major mergers — between Northrop and Grumman, and between Boeing and McDonnell Douglas — joined Raytheon and Litton as the new "big five." The merged Lockheed Martin continued looking beyond defense contracts and formed a joint venture with Boeing in September 1996. Known as the United Space Alliance, or USA, the venture would support NASA's space shuttle program, offering a single prime contractor to consolidate a growing array of disparate subcontracts.

Manned spaceflight and shuttle servicing missions had become almost routine. From 1991 to 1996, NASA had racked up 42 successful shuttle missions. They included the first unclassified Department of Defense mission aboard space shuttle Discovery in April 1991, which included military science experiments, and the first Hubble servicing mission in December 1993, to correct the telescope's faulty optics.

By 1998, Lockheed Martin had also developed the Super Lightweight Tank, lowering the weight of the external tank to about 58,500 pounds (the external tank that had launched Columbia's first mission in 1981 weighed nearly 76,000 pounds). This design change and shift to a lighter aluminum-lithium alloy made it possible for shuttles to carry heavier payloads. The breakthrough was hugely important: It allowed the shuttle, during more than 30 construction and resupply missions starting in 1998, to deliver to orbit the modules and structures that would become the International Space Station.

The space shuttle Atlantis departs the Russian space station Mir during the STS-71 mission, July 4, 1995.

INTERNATIONAL SPACE STATION

First there was Salyut. Then there was Skylab. And as the Russian space station Mir ended its operational life, the global stargazing community prepared for the next incarnation of a workshop in space. Over the previous two decades, humans had made enormous strides toward setting up shop beyond the bounds of Earth, but there was more work to be done.

The key ingredient of the International Space Station is its modularity. It was designed so a vast array of interchangeable components — laboratories, solar arrays, docking ports, cargo bays and living quarters — could all connect to a system of external trusses, allowing the ISS to grow and change over time. But that's not what made the ISS most special.

When the first component was launched in 1998 after more than 20 years of fierce space-based competition, the ISS stood out as the most complex and substantial example of international collaboration ever attempted in space. Lockheed Martin built the ISS's four pairs of electricity-generating solar array wings and thermal radiators, as well as its Trace Containment Control System, an air-filtration system. The company also provides ongoing cargo services for the ISS, managing, supplying and restocking the crew's basic necessities like food, clothing and hygiene products.

Today, at least 15 countries contribute to the effort. Astronauts from more than a dozen countries have visited the ISS. It has grown to the approximate size of an American football field and under the right conditions can be seen by the naked eye. At any given time, an array of government, academic and commercial initiatives are being carried out 240 miles above Earth. The ISS will not be the last of these international efforts to explore and understand space, but the design of the space station allows it to continually evolve as an international laboratory in space.

International Space Station as of March 7, 2011.

UNDERSTANDING EARTH

In May 1996, Clinton outlined a plan to "encourage acceptance and integration of GPS into peaceful civil, commercial and scientific applications worldwide; and to encourage private-sector investment in and use of U.S. GPS technologies and services."[9] Four years later, the U.S. government discontinued its practice of intentionally degrading GPS signals for national security reasons, known as Selective Availability — thereby enhancing its value for both civilian and military users.

Over the years, many organizations have played a role in the refinement of GPS. Lockheed Martin built the GPS IIR series, which launched on July 23, 1997, and ultimately designed and built 21 GPS IIR satellites for the Air Force. Eight of these spacecraft were eventually upgraded and designated GPS IIR-M to enhance performance and reliability for a system that, along with the World Wide Web, came to define the global information infrastructure in the 1990s.

The world was changing. By the late 1990s, new global and domestic threats came in the form of changing, decentralized and often hidden enemies. The Internet allowed for an unprecedented leap in convenience and connection, allowing messages, images and digital files to be sent anywhere in the world in a fraction of a second. It spurred the spread of information on a global scale, and anyone with a computer and a modem could tap into vast stores of knowledge. But it also aided in the coordination of a decentralized threat. A single computer hacker could plant software viruses capable of bringing down complex systems, covering their tracks through electronic encryption. A single, unassuming radical working out of a bedroom in Peshawar or Oklahoma City could tap into nefarious networks, planning and executing violent acts against innocent citizens. This threat did not carry a national flag and could not be defined by clearly demarcated borders. This was a hidden threat, a new generation of guerrilla warfare.

The most clear and disconcerting terrorist threat emerged out of the rubble of the Soviet war in Afghanistan and was stoked by the U.S.-led actions in the Persian Gulf. After the Soviet-backed Afghan government fell, a nationalist group known as the Taliban consolidated influence throughout the region. By 1996, the Taliban controlled most of Afghanistan and provided safe harbor for a rapidly growing network of integrated terrorist cells known as al-Qaida.

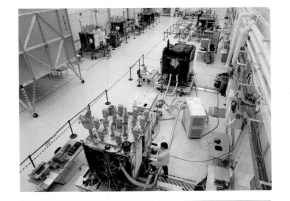

Lockheed Martin's GPS IIR and IIR-M satellites provide positioning, navigation and timing capabilities to American warfighters, NATO allies and civilian users worldwide.

Led by wealthy militant Osama bin Laden, and initially made up of parts of the mujahideen that only recently had opposed the Soviets, al-Qaida aimed to expel Western influence from Muslim countries.

The threat became reality beginning in 1992, with a largely ineffectual attack in Yemen, and in 1993, when a truck bomb was detonated outside New York's World Trade Center. Other al-Qaida truck bombings occurred at U.S. embassies in Kenya and Tanzania in 1998, and 17 naval servicemen were killed in October 2000 when al-Qaida suicide bombers crashed an explosives-laden power boat into the hull of the USS *Cole*. While devastating to many communities, these terrorist attacks did little to prepare the world for the coming storm.

On September 11, 2001, America woke to televised images of smoke pouring from the north tower of New York City's World Trade Center. A commercial jet had crashed into the building. When a second airliner hit the south tower some 15 minutes later, it became clear that this was no freak accident. Both towers collapsed, killing some 3,000 innocent citizens. The horrors of 9/11 ushered in a new age of asymmetric and irregular security threats. Compared to the weaponry of Desert Storm, this was a low-tech attack: America's own civilian aircraft had been transformed into deadly weapons. Numerous individual suicide hijackers, working on behalf of an unforeseen and largely hidden global network, coordinated the attack. Al-Qaida had emerged as the free world's invisible enemy.

Tarnak Farms, near Kandahar, Afghanistan, was one of the major al-Qaida terrorist training camps funded by Osama bin Laden, 2001.

CHAPTER 8

WORLDWIDE NETWORKS

The Advent of Global Security

2001–2012

"THE UNITED STATES IS GRATEFUL THAT MANY NATIONS AND MANY INTERNATIONAL ORGANIZATIONS HAVE ALREADY RESPONDED — WITH SYMPATHY AND WITH SUPPORT. ... PERHAPS THE NATO CHARTER REFLECTS BEST THE ATTITUDE OF THE WORLD: AN ATTACK ON ONE IS AN ATTACK ON ALL."[1]

—PRESIDENT GEORGE W. BUSH

GLOBAL COOPERATION

On July 20, 2001, a pilot flying the Lockheed Martin's X-35B Joint Strike Fighter prototype performed a short takeoff, accelerated to supersonic speed and then descended for a vertical landing. This proof-of-concept system heralded a new generation of multirole fighter aircraft and a new era of collaborative aircraft development.

Lockheed Martin's Joint Strike Fighter, also known as the F-35 Lightning II, is being collaboratively developed by a team of nine nations, whose flags appear on the side of this plane's fuselage. [INSET] Lockheed Martin's X-35A concept demonstrator for the Joint Strike Fighter competition flies over Edwards AFB, Calif., in November 2000. The two X-35 demonstrator aircraft were built at Lockheed Martin's Skunk Works facility and were the prototypes for the F-35 Lightning II.

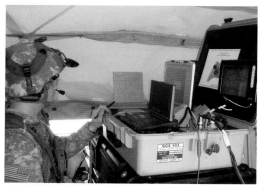

Lockheed Martin's Desert Hawk III small unmanned aircraft system provides the warfighter with an easy-to-use persistent surveillance platform. A portable ground control station with touchscreen laptop allows remote operators to view video transmitted from the air vehicle.

The JSF had been developed in partnership with the United Kingdom and Canada, whose investment helped create the prototype demonstration aircraft. Nine partner countries had agreed to make the JSF part of their air forces — an unprecedented example of global collaboration. First, however, Lockheed Martin had to win the competition to build the plane. While Lockheed Martin perfected its fifth-generation JSF stealth fighter in preparation for the coming competition, a much simpler aircraft prepared to take to the skies.

Launched using a bungee cord, Lockheed Martin's Desert Hawk unmanned aerial vehicle looked more like a toy airplane than a high-tech military platform. "The manual describes the plane as a state-of-the-art composite material, but it's actually got a lot more in common with a Styrofoam cup," said Staff Sgt. Michael Roth.[2]

Though inexpensive and remarkably simple, the remote-controlled Desert Hawk carried color cameras and thermal imagers for aerial surveillance. The UAV's missions could be preprogrammed and altered in flight using a touch-screen laptop. Most impressively, the aircraft could land without human intervention. In the Middle East military operations that occurred following September 11, Lockheed Martin's Desert Hawks discovered weapons caches and antiaircraft artillery while operating in Afghanistan and helped protect U.S. airmen stationed in Iraq. By 2006, British forces had also deployed the updated Desert Hawk III in Iraq and Afghanistan, working with Lockheed Martin to procure additional unmanned aerial vehicles by fall 2010. "The DH III is a fantastic bit of kit," said Staff Sgt. Leighton Davies of the United Kingdom's 47th Regiment Royal Artillery. "It's a company commander's asset that he has with him at all times."[3]

In a new era of global security, Lockheed Martin rose to the challenge, creating technology large and small, complex and simple, manned and unmanned. A new portfolio of land, sea and aerial vehicles soon complemented an ever-expanding technological array, including missile warning and intercept systems, satellites, cyber security and training systems. As military operations confronted complex and rapidly evolving threats worldwide, Lockheed Martin would be called upon to create the indispensable tools of an unstable era.

"TO THOSE WHO WOULD STRIKE AT THE HEART OF FREEDOM'S CITADEL, THERE CAN BE NO SANCTUARY, BUT IT IS ALSO IMPERATIVE THAT AS A NATION WE SECURE THE HOMELAND FROM THE THREAT OF TERRORISM. THE VALUES THAT SUSTAIN AND GUIDE THIS COUNTRY FROM ITS FOUNDING TO THE PRESENT DAY ARE IMMUTABLE, AND NOT SUBJECT TO NEGOTIATION OR COMPROMISE."

— LOCKHEED MARTIN ANNUAL REPORT, 2002

On October 11, 2001, a memorial service on the Pentagon River Parade Field honored those killed and injured during the terrorist attacks on Sept. 11, 2001.

PICKING UP THE PIECES

September 11 was very much like Pearl Harbor 60 years before it. The surprise attack resulted in almost 3,000 deaths, and people in America and around the world grappled with confusion, grief and anger. Terrorist cells — decentralized yet coordinated — were the new primary threat to the United States and its allies. Osama bin Laden was the world's most wanted man.

The impending War on Terror would be fought on many fronts, relying on global diplomacy, reconnaissance and intelligence-gathering, border and homeland defense, and economic sanctions, as well as traditional and innovative military action. Though Afghanistan was initially targeted as the locus of the al-Qaida organization, the technologically savvy enemy and its leaders could be anywhere.

Army UH-60 Blackhawk helicopters fly above a C-130 Hercules at Bagram Air Base, Afghanistan.

INTO AND BEYOND AFGHANISTAN

The scattered al-Qaida network constituted an asymmetric threat, as opposed to the race between superpowers that had dominated the global landscape for most of the 20th century. The United States prepared to confront unfamiliar enemy strategies and tactics, entering an inhospitable territory where the Soviet superpower had recently failed to gain a foothold. When initial attempts at diplomacy failed to elicit cooperation from Afghan leaders, NATO's mutual defense provision was invoked for the first time since the organization's founding. All participating countries as well as non-NATO nations such as Russia and Pakistan joined the fight against the 9/11 perpetrators and countries that supported terrorism.

As with the Gulf War a decade earlier, Operation Enduring Freedom began in the middle of the night with an airstrike on communications, command and control, airfields, and radar facilities. The offensive began with bombing raids in Afghanistan on October 7, 2001. By mid-December, an interim government was established in Kabul. By March 2002, the Taliban and al-Qaida had been ousted from the Afghan capital.

But the conflict was far from over.

OPERATION IRAQI FREEDOM

During his State of the Union address in January 2002, Bush described the nations of Iran, North Korea and Iraq as an "axis of evil," supporting terrorism and developing chemical, biological and nuclear weapons of mass destruction. Saddam Hussein was again targeted by the United States as a central threat with links to al-Qaida. Unlike the 1991 campaign to oust Iraqi invaders from Kuwait, however, the United States prepared to launch a preemptive strike.

With a coordinated air assault set to unleash on Baghdad, Bush shifted the plan at the 11th hour, urged by intelligence that Saddam himself had been geo-located. On March 19, 2003, pilots in Lockheed Martin's F-117 stealth fighters and ship-launched Tomahawk missiles hit the Dora Farm complex outside Baghdad with guided munitions. Though the complex was destroyed, Saddam was nowhere to be found.

The following day, the U.S. aerial assault proceeded as planned, softening key military and communications targets throughout the Iraqi capital. A ground campaign followed. Modernized versions of the F-16 Fighting Falcon, U-2 Dragon Lady recon-naissance plane, the C-130 Hercules and later, the new C-130J Super Hercules also saw active duty in Iraq.

In the early months of the campaign, AH-64 Apache helicopters again took their place as frontline fighters, equipped with a new generation of night vision sensors and thermobaric Hellfire missiles "capable of reaching around corners, striking enemy forces that hide in caves or bunkers and hardened multiroom complexes."[4]

Lockheed Martin is the prime contractor to the U.S. Navy for the Aegis Combat System. The world's most capable naval defense system, Aegis can simultaneously attack land and sea targets while automatically protecting the fleet against aircraft and missiles. During Operation Iraqi Freedom, Aegis-equipped Guided Missile Cruisers like the USS Princeton solidified their reputation as floating shields for coalition forces.

THE BEST OFFENSE IS A GOOD DEFENSE

SHIELDS IN THE SKY

Back in 1984, during a series of Homing Overlay Experiments over the Pacific Ocean, Lockheed pioneered "hit to kill" defensive missiles. That initial breakthrough paved the way for the next-generation PAC-3 Missile, the world's most advanced and powerful terminal air defense missile. The Patriot system now had the ability to counter new missile-launched chemical and biological weapon threats, as well as tactical ballistic missiles and enemy aircraft.

On March 20, 2003, the wail of warning sirens at a key command operations center in Kuwait announced the approach of an incoming enemy missile. The effects of a direct hit would be catastrophic, crippling the command center responsible for coordinating the offensive. Inside the command center, team members put on their protective masks and waited anxiously. As the missiles bore down on their target, the walls began to rumble. The roof began to

shake. Then came the shriek of two nearby missiles — a pair of Lockheed Martin PAC-3s — ascending to their rapidly approaching target. A loud explosion erupted overhead, marking the first successful PAC-3 engagement.

The PAC-3's success helped prove the value of a layered missile defense shield. While PAC-3 defended against tactical missiles and aircraft, Lockheed Martin's Terminal High Altitude Area Defense (THAAD) system, first manufactured in 2000, was designed to intercept incoming missiles in the upper atmosphere and near-space at a greater distance from the ground, where the fallout from collisions wouldn't affect targeted areas. THAAD, PAC-3 and Aegis together make up an integrated missile defense shield, protecting against a wide range of potential global threats.

Those systems are woven together by a central IT network, developed by a Lockheed Martin-led "National Team" of

Lockheed Martin's Terminal High Altitude Area Defense (THAAD) system was designed to intercept missiles farther from Earth to minimize the effects back on the ground.

aerospace firms, that links satellites, sensors and defensive batteries into a common command and control network. Called C2BMC, the system creates a worldwide missile defense command center where military leaders can monitor and respond to threats 24/7.

The Medium Extended Air Defense System (MEADS), a versatile and mobile missile shield built for next-generation threats, is currently being cooperatively developed by the United States, Italy and Germany. The fully armored yet light-weight vehicle at the heart of MEADS is designed to move swiftly alongside military units, protecting soldiers on cross-country marches through tough terrain.

The combination of multiple missile defense batteries provides a highly accurate, layered defense, creating a mobile shield in the sky designed to protect American interests near home and across the globe.

The Command, Control, Battle Management and Communications system integrates and interconnects widely dispersed missile defense systems, including Aegis ships, ground-based interceptors and Patriot missile defense systems. The layered architecture of C2BMC allows rapid decision-making by the national command authorities during missile attacks.

Currently in development, MEADS offers 360-degree radar protection, launching its new defensive missiles — an advanced PAC-3 MSE — from a near vertical position, greatly improving coverage and intercept range. Equally critical, MEADS offers "plug-and-fight" capabilities — the ability to instantly interconnect with key U.S. and allied sensors, radars and communications systems in a given area.

ARROWHEADS IN FLIGHT

Helicopters were crucial to Operation Iraqi Freedom's campaign in mountainous and urban areas alike. But 12 American helicopters had been shot down during the first three months of action, all while flying at low altitudes.

Since the Vietnam War, helicopter pilots were trained to fly "low and fast," a technique that helped them avoid radar-guided missiles and antiaircraft artillery. The urban areas of Iraq, however, required new tactics. Insurgents set buildings on fire, creating veils of smoke that blinded low-flying Apaches, making them easier targets for rocket-propelled grenades and shoulder-launched surface-to-air missiles. The Apache needed a new set of eyes — and that's exactly what Lockheed Martin was about to deliver.

Building on the Apache Helicopter's late 1970s vintage electro-optical targeting and navigation system, Lockheed Martin created a modernized targeting and navigational optics system named Arrowhead. By June 2005, Arrowhead-equipped Apaches could hover at higher altitudes and farther from targets, launching Hellfire missiles while staying beyond the reach of insurgent antiaircraft fire. Arrowhead also helped pilots avoid flying into wires and power lines — an ever-present threat in urban warfare. The Apache could see all.

With the successful installation of more than 1,000 Arrowhead systems in Apaches by 2012, Lockheed Martin began developing new high-definition cameras to bolster the Apache's already impressive vision during daylight hours, making the chopper equally effective day and night.

"The M-TADS/PNVS is a game-changer on the battlefield," said Colonel Shane Openshaw, U.S. Army Project Manager for the Apache. "An Apache equipped with M-TADS/PNVS is the most lethal and survivable attack helicopter in the world."[5]

The Arrowhead program — also known as the Modernized Target Acquisition Designation Sight/Pilot Night Vision System (M-TADS/PNVS) — used advanced infrared sensors, allowing pilots to see twice as far at night and through smoke and inclement weather.

DRIVING FORCES

LOCKHEED MARTIN'S AUTONOMOUS LAND VEHICLES

On May 31, 1985, a strange-looking, 10-foot-tall, blue-and-white vehicle appeared on a narrow dirt road outside of Denver, creeping along at a snail's pace in the shadow of the Rockies. A large, roof-mounted, closed-circuit camera peeked out from the top of its boxy frame while three diesel engines carefully propelled it along at a crawl of 3 mph. Having traveled just over a half mile, cautiously toeing the center line of a narrow road, the vehicle came to a halt in front of a group of 80 military and academic officials gathered to witness the landmark test.

No driver emerged from the Autonomous Land Vehicle. Incredibly, the vehicle had driven itself. Inside the ALV, six racks of computers, all programmed by Martin Marietta engineers, had used images from the rooftop camera to safely steer without human assistance, paving the way for revolutionary advances in unmanned robotic transports.

A collaborative effort of Martin Marietta, academic institutions and the Defense Advanced Research Projects Agency, the ALV was created in just nine months, establishing a viable platform for development of more advanced autonomous navigation systems.

The principal aim of this new initiative — called Convoy Active Safety Technology — was to increase safety for military drivers. If soldiers driving in the middle of a convoy suddenly came under enemy fire, they could simply press a button and watch as their vehicles locked on to and closely followed the movements of another truck, giving them the opportunity to better defend themselves.

Taking the concept one step further, Lockheed Martin began development in 2006 of a more advanced unmanned combat vehicle called the Squad Support Mission System, which could track the movements of a single soldier, opening up a dazzling new range of possibilities, including cargo movement for small units, casualty evacuation and backup power support.

In 2011, when the six-wheeled, all-terrain SMSS made its combat debut in Afghanistan, it quickly earned a nickname, *the Ox*, for its strength and resourcefulness as well as its ability to haul 1,000 pounds of supplies over rough terrain.

The SMSS would be used in Afghanistan, supplying special operations units pinned down in remote locations as well as transporting equipment and supplies to soldiers working on construction projects throughout the region.

"WHERE WE ARE IN TERMS OF UNMANNED AERIAL VEHICLES IS ABOUT THE SAME PLACE WE WERE WITH BIPLANES RIGHT AFTER WORLD WAR I."[6]

— AIR FORCE LT. GEN. DAVID A. DEPTULA (RET.)

AIRBORNE EVOLUTION

The Kettering Aerial Torpedo, the world's first unmanned aerial vehicle, was a remarkable piece of technology. Known as the Bug, this UAV was guided toward its target by a system of preset internal controls. After flying more than 75 miles at close to 120 mph, an electrical circuit closed automatically, shutting off the engine. The wings were then released, causing the vehicle to plunge to Earth. The Bug's 180-pound explosives payload detonated on impact. The year: 1918.

Unmanned aircraft have come a long way since then.

UAVs are swiftly becoming essential components of U.S. and allied operations around the globe. The ability to cover ground, whether measured by range or by endurance, is a defining characteristic. The exponential leaps in computing power, advanced flight controls and materials over the past 20 years allow even small unmanned systems to carry useful payloads.

As the use of UAVs expanded, Lockheed Martin contributed to the wave of unmanned technology in transport and reconnaissance aircraft. As the Desert Hawk patrolled the skies of Iraq and Afghanistan, the unmanned transport helicopter K-MAX was deployed to Afghanistan in November 2011, and a month later became the first unmanned helicopter to deliver cargo in theater. K-MAX's deployment has been extended twice, and the U.S. Marine Corps recently requested K-MAX stay in theater through the end of Operation Enduring Freedom.

Throughout its history, Lockheed Martin has been involved with unmanned aircraft, starting with the Bug, which was developed by legacy company Dayton-Wright.

In the 1960s, Skunk Works developed the ramjet-powered, high-altitude D-21 reconnaissance drone sitting atop an A-12.

Developed by Lockheed Martin and Kaman Aerospace, K-MAX protects soldiers by reducing the number of truck resupply convoys and their troop escorts, which are frequent targets of improvised explosive devices and insurgent attacks.

Satellite image by GeoEye

Satellite image by GeoEye

Orbiting more than 400 miles over the Earth, Lockheed Martin's IKONOS satellite captured images of Iranian nuclear facilities in Natanz and Arak in 2002 and 2004, showing evidence of the country's attempts at expanding and camouflaging the locations.

PERIPHERAL VISION

While the growing use of UAVs allowed military forces to track and sometimes eliminate elusive terrorist threats, keeping eyes on "nonstate terrorists" was not the only global priority during the first decade of the 21st century. Countering potentially hostile nation-states such as North Korea and Iran was of vital importance to avoid a repeat of Cold War tensions in the new millennium.

In October 2006, North Korea detonated its first nuclear device, taking a major step toward realizing a nuclear program it had been pursuing for decades. While the explosion was reportedly smaller than expected, the international community condemned the actions of North Korea and its longtime dictator, Kim Jong Il, imposing military and economic sanctions.

Iran was also accelerating its nuclear aspirations. Despite U.N. sanctions, newly elected Iranian president Mahmoud Ahmadinejad pursued production at uranium enrichment facilities in 2005.

The ongoing wars in Iraq and Afghanistan, coupled with rising threats from Iran and North Korea, meant that the next generation of global security technology needed to be not only superior but also flexible, affordable and adaptable to a rapidly changing world.

NEXT-GENERATION FIGHTERS

The Air Force had realized by the 1980s that it would eventually need to replace its distinguished but aging F-15 Eagle air superiority fighter with a fighter that would combine stealth, advanced avionics and super-maneuverability that could deal with new and emerging threats worldwide. After a "dogfight" with a competing design, Lockheed won the competition to design and build this new, superior fighter in 1991, and the aircraft was first flown in 1997. After a thorough test and evaluation phase, the Lockheed Martin F-22 Raptor, described as an air dominance fighter, was declared ready for combat in 2005.

The single-seat, twin-engine fighter could soar 10 miles high and fly at supersonic speeds for extended periods of time. It could accelerate quickly and execute razor-sharp turns — even at high speeds. It carried weapons for striking both airborne and ground-based targets. And it was equipped with stealth technology that enabled it to operate virtually undetected by radar.

On May 5, 2012, the last two F-22 Raptors departed from Marietta, Ga., for their new home in Alaska, completing the world's first operational fifth-generation fleet.

The Air Force has described the F-22 as "unmatched by any known or projected fighter."[7] The National Aeronautic Association awarded Lockheed Martin the Collier Trophy, American aviation's most prestigious award, for "designing, testing and operating the revolutionary F-22 Raptor, providing total air dominance for America's future."[8]

FULL SPEED AHEAD

After September 11, a new class of warship was conceived to respond to shallow water, or "littoral," threats. Designed to complement the U.S. Navy's fleet of Aegis destroyers, Lockheed Martin's Littoral Combat Ship "is envisioned to be a networked, agile, stealthy surface combatant capable of defeating anti-access and asymmetric threats in the littorals."[9]

Two versions of the LCS will replace several ships in the current naval fleet. The USS *Freedom*, the first of the Lockheed Martin-built class of LCS ships, was built in partnership with Marinette Marine Corp., a subsidiary of Italian-based Fincantieri SpA, and delivered to the Navy in 2008. It completed its first deployment in 2010, two years ahead of schedule, and in 2013 deployed to Singapore.

On March 31, 2010, the crew of an MH-60S Seahawk helicopter lifted off from the USS *Freedom* and headed after a speedboat slicing through the Eastern Pacific. The speedboat carried suspected drug smugglers, and the agile LCS also gave chase. After firing a few warning shots into the ocean, fire from a sniper onboard the chopper hit the

speedboat's outboard engines, disabling it just in time for *Freedom's* crew to intercept and board the suspected drug-running vessel. *Freedom* crews seized about a ton of cocaine and arrested the four smugglers on board. This was the fourth group of drug runners nabbed by the LCS in just over two months at sea, bringing the total haul to about five tons of illegal drugs. "*Freedom* completed all operational tasking in superb fashion," said Rear Adm. Vic Guillory. "Its inherent design capabilities of sprint speed, shallow draft and modularity were key enablers in accomplishing the counter-illicit trafficking mission. Every sailor on the ship . . . helped move our 21st century Navy forward."[10]

The LCS design can be reconfigured and adapted to meet the needs of naval forces around the globe. The international design — known as the Multi-Mission Combat Ship — features the proven Aegis combat system with the MK 41 Vertical Launching System.

The F-35 Lightning II meets its namesake, the Lockheed P-38 Lightning, at Edwards Air Force Base, 2011.

GLOBAL COOPERATION

Oct. 26, 2001, was Decision Day. Secretary of the Air Force James Roche, standing at a podium in Washington, D.C., prepared to announce the winner of the single greatest airplane design competition in history. The Joint Strike Fighter contest had pitted Boeing against Lockheed Martin in a winner-take-all competition. The goal was to create a plane capable of fulfilling the collective needs of the Air Force, Navy and Marine Corps.

A truly global fighter, the JSF had been developed in partnership with the United Kingdom and Canada, whose initial investment helped both competitor companies create a prototype demonstration aircraft. Boeing offered its X-32, with its delta wing design and a central air intake under the nose. Lockheed Martin, by contrast, offered its X-35, with sleek angular wings and a cutting-edge lift-fan engine for vertical landings.

The quest to create a fighter capable of taking off and landing in confined spaces had been a decades-long pursuit on both sides of the Atlantic. As early as 1954, Lockheed was busy designing experimental vertical takeoff and landing, or VTO, aircraft. But unlike the British Harrier, which was limited in both range and payload capabilities, the X-35B and its short takeoff and vertical landing system, or STOVL, offered both vertical landing and supersonic dash capability in one, creating a stealthy, fast fighter capable of carrying advanced weaponry.

In the end, the advanced capabilities of the X-35 carried the day. "On the basis of strengths, weaknesses and degrees of risk of the program," Roche said, "it is our conclusion ... that the Lockheed Martin team is the winner of the Joint Strike Fighter program on a best-value basis."[11]

It was official. Lockheed Martin had been given the green light to create the most technologically advanced aircraft ever devised. With primary funding from the United States, as well as major contributions from the United Kingdom, Italy, the Netherlands, Australia, Canada, Turkey, Norway and Denmark, three F-35 variants were designed, with modifications to meet the particular needs of each military branch. All three were supersonic stealth fighters, but the F-35C Navy version would be optimized for carrier operations. The Marine Corps' F-35B was built to execute a short takeoff from amphibious assault ships, engage targets on the ground, and land vertically back on the ship. The Air Force's F-35A — the variant most allies will fly — is designed for conventional runways and features an internal gun.

Each set of stealth aircraft would share more than 60 percent of its respective parts, making all of the fighters less costly to build and repair. This was a key provision, as the Department of Defense envisioned the F-35 as a replacement for five other fighters: the Air Force's F-16 and A-10, the Navy's early model F/A-18s, and the Marine Corps' (and Royal Navy/Royal Air Force's) AV-8B Harrier and F/A-18C/D.

An age of global security demanded global cooperation. The first official F-35 fighter received its nickname — Lightning II — and was rolled out on Feb. 20, 2006. Sourcing, manufacturing and funding by many different countries made the F-35 possible, giving all partner nations a single fighter aircraft with common logistics and maintenance infrastructure. The future of allied global security had its new frontline fighter.

Using energy generated by the aircraft's single engine, a swiveling jet pipe capable of rotating 95 degrees in 2.5 seconds can redirect the engine thrust downward, while the lift fan, behind the cockpit, produces 40,000 pounds of vertical thrust. Here, an F-35B STOVL aircraft hovers during a night test flight, Dec. 13, 2012.

The F-35 continues to make progress and meet its benchmarks, flying at supersonic speeds in 2008 and showing off its full vertical landing capabilities in 2010. By the summer of 2011, pilot training had begun at Elgin Air Force Base in Florida. According to current estimates, some 4,500 F-35 aircraft could see action around the globe.

CHAPTER 9

CYBERSPACE

Ushering a Connected World Into the Future

2001–2012

"OUR FATES AND FORTUNES ARE LINKED AS PEOPLES, AS COUNTRIES, AND AS REGIONS. SO AT LOCKHEED MARTIN WE RECOGNIZE THAT GLOBAL SECURITY IS HUMAN SECURITY, WHICH COMES DOWN TO THE BASICS PEOPLE DEPEND ON IN THEIR DAILY LIVES."[1]

—ROBERT J. STEVENS, EXECUTIVE CHAIRMAN, LOCKHEED MARTIN

REAL CHALLENGES MEET VIRTUAL SOLUTIONS

At the dawn of the new millennium, cyberspace quickly established itself as global security's newest frontier. It became a proving ground, a virtual world where technologies and tactics alike are put to the test. It became a factory, a digital assembly line where designs are tried out, tweaked and

The NexGen Cyber Innovation and Technology Center (NexGen) is a world-class center designed for cyber research and development, customer and partner collaboration, and innovation. It is one of the newest additions to Lockheed Martin's portfolio of research, development and testing facilities. [INSET] The future is now. No longer the subject of science fiction, immersive virtual reality is a powerful manufacturing tool that is revolutionizing the way we design and build modern spacecraft and aircraft.

Dubbed "the Lighthouse" for the iconic 40-foot replica of a 19th-century lighthouse located in its expansive atrium, the Lockheed Martin Center for Innovation is a beacon for collaborative physical and virtual simulations between Lockheed Martin and its U.S. government, international, academic and industry partners.

perfected without ever turning a wrench. And it became a battlefield, an invisible line of trenches where hackers and defenders square off at the speed of light. The dawn of the cyber age accelerated an already dizzying rate of change, and brought with it dazzling new opportunities and dangerous new threats. As governments sought to apply virtual solutions to their very real challenges, Lockheed Martin evolved to stay ahead of the game.

Central to this strategy was the creation of the Lockheed Martin Center for Innovation. Built in 2005 and known as "the Lighthouse," the 65,000-square-foot facility in Hampton Roads, Va., embodies a collaborative synergy of customers and analysts, of high-tech and human psychology.

The Lighthouse uses advanced simulations to offer manufacturers, military troops, first responders and IT experts a glimpse at possible futures. Customers can simulate flying an F-35 Lightning II in a major combat operation without burning jet fuel. They can mimic a Humvee's journey through an urban battlefield without placing troops in harm's way. They can model a catastrophic flood scenario and determine the best rescue scenario without wasting water or damaging property.

In the new security landscape, global defense increasingly requires Lockheed Martin to use technology to create visible, virtual and augmented-reality training tools; to secure IT infrastructure while developing new tools to identify and thwart cyber attacks; and to examine Earth from above while exploring the deeper reaches of space.

SKYBOUND VIRTUAL TOURS

In many ways, Lockheed Martin's commitment to digital and virtual training began just before the turn of the millennium. When the updated C-130J Super Hercules entered service in 1999, former Marine Corps C-130 loadmaster Lee Wiegand recalled the deer-in-the-headlights look of new crew members when he ushered them into the cavernous aircraft. "They're faced with hundreds of pieces of equipment they have to learn," he said. "They're absolutely lost that first time."[2] So Wiegand tapped an unconventional source to help him speed and simplify the training process for C-130 crews: online real estate listings.

Lee Wiegand's early virtual tour training helped C-130 aircrews achieve mission readiness.

He had moved to Little Rock, Ark., from North Carolina in early 2005 and had looked at real estate listings online with his wife. Many of these listings included virtual tours. As it turned out, virtually touring the interior of a C-130 was not so different from an online walkthrough of a split-level Tudor. The off-the-shelf software cost $750, and Wiegand's team members substituted photos of the inside of a C-130, tagging pieces of equipment the crew members needed to learn. The resemblance to a video game was intentional. Young crew members quickly took to competing with other teams for bragging rights, speeding the training process and making it more enjoyable.

Pushing the training concept further meant activating the virtual world beyond a static situation. To truly tap into the human psyche, Lockheed Martin had to simulate complex situations and train soldiers to expect the unexpected.

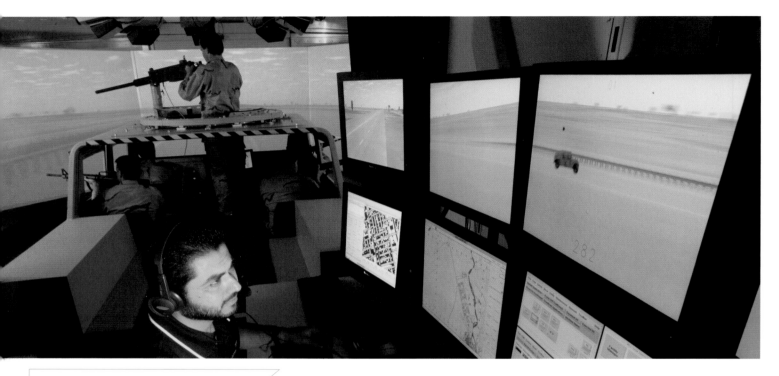

Using input from the military, realistic scenarios of insurgent attacks were programmed into the scenes, testing soldiers' reactions to everything from roadside bombings to sniper attacks. With VCCT, soldiers could fire back using special laser-pulse machine guns, while others attempted to establish communications amid the deafening sounds of gunfire and explosions.

ANTICIPATING THE ENEMY

In 2004, rates of convoy-related casualties in Iraq were rising, largely due to roadside improvised explosive devices and land mines hidden beneath the desert sands. U.S. soldiers needed new technology to help protect them overseas, and they needed it fast.

The answer came from employees at Lockheed Martin's facilities in Orlando, who conceived and created in just 60 days a revolutionary combat simulator that would help keep troops safe by faithfully re-creating the rigors of warfare.

Before the advent of Lockheed Martin's Virtual Combat Convoy Trainer (VCCT) in 2004, U.S. soldiers had to rely on classroom lectures and videos to prepare them for the complex logistical convoy operations that awaited them overseas. The VCCT changed that. By mounting a Humvee in a room lined with oversized monitors, the VCCT created the illusion that soldiers were driving through arid desert terrain and urban areas. When explosions occurred onscreen, hydraulics simulated the blast, testing drivers' ability to safely steer their vehicles upon impact. Most impressive of all, each simulator fit inside a trailer, allowing the VCCT to be quickly shipped overseas and easily deployed to military sites across the globe.

"The first year, we put about 100,000 troops through simulations," said Chester Kennedy, a Lockheed Martin vice president of engineering. "And a lot of us still have emails from soldiers that sent back notes saying, 'You saved my life.'"[3]

As combat simulations evolved, Lockheed Martin brought the benefits of virtual training to a novel area: industrial manufacturing.

IMMERSIVE ENGINEERING

In 2005, engineers at Lockheed Martin's Human Immersive Lab in Fort Worth, Texas, had begun making design changes to the F-35 Lightning II in an entirely new way. Instead of physically creating modifications and add-ons — an expensive and labor-intensive process — engineers crafted digital parts and tweaked designs in a virtual workspace. They strapped on virtual reality goggles, slipped on gloves and bodysuits with special sensors, and entered their own virtual garage, where they could test the F-35's capabilities.

The risk of damaging expensive aircraft components disappeared. The need to create expensive physical mockups was a worry of the past. And when issues were discovered, fixes could be implemented in a fraction of the time needed in the real world. Working on just one project, the F-35, HIL engineers saved Lockheed Martin more than $100 million — a 15-fold return on the company's immersive engineering investment.

And if immersive training could provide value for aircraft manufacturing and maintenance, why not apply the technology to the typically high-cost arena of space systems manufacturing and integration?

Lockheed Martin technicians wear motion-tracking sensors (small white nodes) as they mime aircraft carrier deck tasks. Based on data from the sensors, captured by an array of sensitive motion-tracking cameras (red glowing squares), the movements of the technicians are digitized and converted to animated "avatars" in various task-specific simulations.

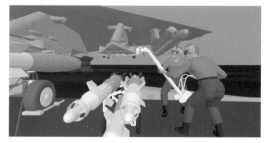

The Human Immersive Lab helped ensure that the design for the underwing fuel drain on the F-35 gave technicians access even when the aircraft is parked tail-over-water on an aircraft carrier. "A one-hour work session can save a retrofit that might cost millions of dollars if caught too late," said Ray Harbor, carrier integration lead for the F-35's Basing and Ship Suitability project.[4]

On January 24, 2011, Lockheed Martin's Space Systems Company in Littleton, Colo., debuted the dynamic Collaborative Human Immersive Lab, in which engineers could not only tweak satellite designs but also moonlight as virtual architects. By slipping on their 3D glasses and motion-sensor suits, designers could enter a virtual mock-up of the company's new production facility and make key alterations to its layout, rearranging the space between workstations and limiting the number of times delicate satellite parts had to be physically moved during testing. The creation of a more efficient work environment led to the development of virtual training seminars on how to properly assemble multimillion-dollar hardware.

CREATING VIRTUAL WORLDS

The Virtual World Labs started out in 2008 as an informal group of engineers and designers tasked with brainstorming how to use immersive technology across the company. Few could predict what they would achieve in just four years.

In 2009, Lockheed Martin won a Department of Defense contract to help develop the innovative Infantry Immersion Trainer (IIT), an "augmented reality" simulator blending the digital and physical worlds. Rather than wearing a fully immersive virtual reality headset — placing the human user into a fully digital or simulated world — augmented reality brought digital elements into the human, real-world environment.

Housed in an old tomato packing plant at Camp Pendleton, Calif., the IIT uses concrete floors and sparse walls that are transformed into a physical re-creation of a modern urban combat environment, including a marketplace and several homes. Crafted according to the accounts of soldiers operating in Fallujah and Basra, this workspace is no video game. It offers hands-on combat tactics training as well as an immersive experience that readies trainees for the emotional pressures of combat. Small squads of soldiers wearing 3D glasses and sensors roam through a set made to resemble an Afghan town. As the squad surveys the physical space through their glasses, they also see interactive holographic "avatars" and simulated battlefield effects, all programmed to provide the illusion of actual combat.

"The objective at the end of the day is for a Marine — facing live combat for the first time — to have already experienced numerous engagements of equivalent intensity but without equal consequences," concluded a September 2009 study by the Naval

Built on Microsoft's popular Flight Simulator engine, Lockheed Martin's Prepar3D is a stunningly accurate multipurpose simulator capable of re-creating the rigors of flight and offering pilot training at a fraction of the cost of professional lessons. Prepar3D is not a game so much as a budget-friendly flight-training program, just one step below the high-end simulators Lockheed Martin creates for the military. The technical and graphic upgrades in Prepar3D are numerous, including realistic new weather effects, painstaking re-creations of actual cockpit designs and an emphasis on real-world physics.

Research Advisory Committee, "so that his first battles, the battles that harden and make him vastly more likely to survive, are virtual."[5]

PROTECTING THE GRID

Since the dawn of global computer networks, there have been both hackers and defenders, those seeking to infiltrate systems and those charged with protecting them — a kind of digital chess match, played out on an invisible game board of computer code created by unseen adversaries. Through much of the 1990s, viruses and antivirus programs battled it out as individual hackers sought to exploit network weaknesses and take down or manipulate key systems.

But in 2003, cyber security specialists at Lockheed Martin, the largest provider of information technology to the federal government, began to encounter attacks

unlike any they had ever seen — new, more coordinated threats launched by teams of intruders who worked systematically, day after day, to target narrow vulnerabilities. These attacks, labeled Advanced Persistent Threats, proved to be a turning point in the history of cyber security. Lockheed Martin joined its customers in working toward eliminating the advantages network aggressors held over network defenders.

Prior to the advent of Advanced Persistent Threat attacks, cyber security specialists focused on using defensive off-the-shelf commercial software — constantly installing new patches and programs to protect a system's hardware and portals from known threats. But commercial software proved futile against the more sophisticated attacks by APT intruders. Whereas individual hackers might create suspicious-looking emails easily detectable by filters, APT intruders crafted startlingly realistic emails that could include forged signatures from executives and attachments disguised to look like standard correspondence and files.

Organized, well-funded and well-trained, these intruders were focused on deeply mining vital networks and poaching the most sensitive economic, intellectual, strategic and military data.

A virtual scenario is monitored from the control room at the Office of Naval Research Infantry Immersion Trainer, while U.S. Marines confront avatars and must assess unique threats during a room-clearing simulation.

Following the 2003 attacks, Lockheed Martin began cataloging and analyzing data from the attacks, looking for patterns in their origin and tactics. The aim was to burrow into the minds of adversaries and then compartmentalize the attacks into distinctive campaigns, each of which could be modeled and tested to see how Lockheed Martin's defenses could best disrupt them. "It's not unlike what the FBI does when a bomb explodes," said Charles Croom, Lockheed Martin's vice president of cyber security solutions. "They go back and do forensics on the bomb. They can often identify who made the bomb based on the way it was built and how it was used, identifying key signatures."[6]

Lockheed Martin pioneered a new defensive strategy called the Cyber Kill Chain,™ which creates customized plans for improving cyber security by analyzing the methods used by adversaries to successfully breach a network, from monitoring a network and building an intrusion weapon to spotting vulnerabilities and implementing the attack. "It really is a chess match," said Chandra McMahon, vice president and chief information security officer of Lockheed Martin. "We make a move and they make a move. We watch. We analyze. We might even let them do something, so we can better understand our adversaries' strategies. But now we're able to see the whole chessboard."[7]

Since 2000, Lockheed Martin has supported NORAD and the U.S. Strategic Command by integrating 40 different systems for air and missile warnings under the Integrated Space Command and Control program.

SAFE AND SECURE

As the chess match intensified, so did the need to secure all aspects of the nation's information infrastructure. After the 9/11 attacks, the newly formed Transportation Security Administration turned to Lockheed Martin to help upgrade security at the nation's airports.

In support of the TSA, Lockheed Martin developed a curriculum and delivered comprehensive classroom and computer-based training to more than 44,000 federal screeners. The company also oversaw a redesign of checkpoints and security operations at the nation's 429 airports in 2002.

The company's homeland security efforts extended to law enforcement, as well. Before July 28, 1999, when Lockheed Martin introduced its Integrated Automated Fingerprint Identification System (IAFIS) to the FBI, fingerprinting was both tedious and imprecise. To run a check on a suspect's fingerprints, police departments had to mail ink-blotted cards to the FBI, which sifted by hand through a catalog of a million index cards, taking up to two months to find a potential match.

With IAFIS, that same fingerprint request could, with the push of a button, be handled in 15 minutes. The introduction of IAFIS — which stores a mix of fingerprints, criminal histories, mug shots and electronic images — forever changed the speed and accuracy with which law-enforcement agencies could fight crime. Fingerprints for a man arrested for loitering in Florida, for instance, quickly revealed an outstanding warrant for murder in California.

By 2012, the average volume for IAFIS was 131,568 searches a day, a number Lockheed Martin hopes to dwarf with the introduction of its new system, dubbed Next Generation Identification (NGI), which is capable of performing 650,000 fingerprint checks per day at an astounding 99 percent accuracy rate. Within five days after NGI went live on February 25, 2011, it had already made 910 new identification matches that the old system could not, adding yet another cutting-edge crime-fighting weapon to the FBI's already impressive arsenal.

With updated features rolling out at regular intervals through 2018, NGI will store and compare a wide variety of new data, from partial prints and palm impressions to tattoos and unique facial markers, offering law enforcement agencies a vast catalogue of search engines.

ACCELERATING GOVERNMENT SERVICES

Population growth crept along steadily for thousands of years. And then, during the Industrial Revolution, the graph spiked. In less than 75 years, the global population tripled, and by 1999 the number reached 6 billion. Delivering services to an ever-growing population is now more challenging and more important than at any time in human history.

Information technology quickly proved its value in making government services more effective and efficient. As the U.S. government's No. 1 provider of information technology solutions for 19 straight years, Lockheed Martin has helped agencies transform the way they deliver a wide range of vital services to citizens.

In the year 2000, the Lockheed Martin-designed Data Capture System 2000 set speed and accuracy records for the U.S. census, processing over a billion pages with more than 99 percent accuracy. For the 2010 census, Lockheed Martin topped its own record, pushing its accuracy rate to 99.98 percent, well above the goal of 99.80 percent. The Lockheed Martin team slashed costs by hundreds of millions of dollars while processing a record 167 million forms. The team also finished the job in six months, meeting the U.S. Census Bureau's aggressive schedule.

Lockheed Martin leverages its census expertise in other countries, as well. It was the prime census contractor for the United Kingdom in 2001 and 2011, and processed census forms for the Canadian government in 2006 and 2011. The 2006 Canadian census was the first in North America to give citizens the choice of submitting information to a secure Internet site.

SIGNED, SEALED, DELIVERED

While the Internet has changed the nature of human correspondence, the U.S. Postal Service is still a primary vehicle for sending packages all over the world. Since the late 1980s, Lockheed Martin Postal Systems designed, built and distributed to the USPS a system of small parcel and bundle sorters. The system automates the sorting of packages, bundled letters and magazines. This high level of automation has allowed the USPS to "constantly improve service while maintaining the lowest postage rates in the industrialized world."[8]

ORCHESTRATING THE AIR

When the FAA again needed to modernize its systems, Lockheed Martin answered the call. The User Resource Evaluation Tool, which was operational in seven traffic control sites by 2002, provided conflict detection systems between aircraft and enhanced electronic flight data available to air traffic controllers. By the mid-2000s, Lockheed Martin had also implemented Advanced Technology Oceanic Procedures, with centers in New York, Anchorage and Oakland, Calif., covering airspace over the Atlantic and Pacific oceans.

En Route Automation Modernization represents the latest phase in the evolution of the nation's air traffic control system, with Lockheed Martin serving as prime contractor. These systems move air traffic control away from the original model of a "highway in the sky" toward more flexibility and freedom in commercial aviation while making flying faster, cheaper and more environmentally friendly than ever.

Postal carriers once had to manually sort their mail into an efficient delivery sequence before going out on their routes. Lockheed Martin's Carrier Sequence Barcode Sorter automated this process, drastically accelerating mail delivery.

A collection of technological innovations brought together in the systemwide ERAM upgrade will help airlines fly more efficient routes, save fuel and reduce emissions, including decibel levels, across the country. Already running 24/7 in the Seattle and Salt Lake City air traffic control centers, ERAM will be rolled out to all 20 centers over the next several years.

NEXGEN

While advanced technology helped law enforcement agencies such as the FBI more quickly locate criminal individuals in the real world, the growing threat of unseen criminals operating in the digital world became more prominent in 2009, when a series of coordinated cyber attacks in July caused government, media and financial websites across the United States and South Korea to overload and crash. Around the same time, another series of APT attacks known as Operation Aurora targeted some 30 U.S. companies. It quickly became apparent that the threat was real and immediate, and required serious action.

With cyber attacks increasing at an alarming rate, Lockheed Martin created the NexGen Cyber Innovation and Technology Center. NexGen was a new breed of R&D facility, a high-tech laboratory for collaboration, experimentation and development. It showcased collaborative work areas, a green IT data center and cloud-computing capabilities, all designed to help thwart cyber attacks from traditional hackers as well as well-equipped, trained and organized attackers. At NexGen, Lockheed Martin offered specialized training to help cyber analysts repel new attacks while allowing them to test products from members of the Cyber Security Alliance on Lockheed Martin's Global Cyber Innovation Range, simulating a range of attacks and defensive countermeasures.

Soon enough, the simulations became reality.

In May 2011, the Lockheed Martin Cyber Kill Chain framework was put to the test. A team of intruders launched one of the most aggressive and sophisticated attacks Lockheed Martin has ever faced. Unable to breach the company's secure network through traditional means, the intruders adopted a back-channel strategy. But after having monitored the intruders for over a year, Lockheed Martin was able to identify a pattern in the use of credentials, anticipate their moves and shut down the intrusion before any data was lost. "It was an example in which all of our systems and all of our capabilities operated exactly the way we wanted them to," Chandra McMahon said. "For us, it was just another good day at work, doing our jobs, protecting the network."[9]

Further collaborations introduced at NexGen yielded an array of new solutions, each designed to help government agencies and corporations defend their networks and systems against the Advanced Persistent Threats without having to make major financial commitments. Two of those products, LM StarVision™ and Palisade,™ converted complex technologies into serviceable products, allowing clients to detect threats earlier and more easily defend against attacks.

As attackers get smarter and better-organized, international cooperation will be key to countering them. Lockheed Martin has opened NexGen facilities in the United Kingdom and Australia, expanding the company's commitment to cyber security around the globe.

Cyber crime is not the only major threat to a digitally interconnected world. While the future of data management and cyber security may be based in "the cloud," high-tech eyes from a much higher vantage point continue to keep watch over the Earth, helping to analyze the past and predict the future of our environment.

The success and resiliency of the Cyber Kill Chain initiative has proved to be a monumental paradigm shift for cyber defense programs across the world. While 80 percent of conventional cyber threats can still be countered by using carefully chosen defensive software and programs, Lockheed Martin's Cyber Kill Chain has become a leading strategy for countering Advanced Persistent Threats.

SATELLITE SMARTS

  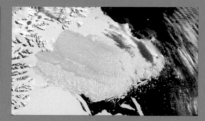

With remote sensors developed by U.S., Canadian and Japanese companies, Lockheed Martin's Terra satellite can "measure the Earth's carbon dioxide, land surfaces, rainforests, clouds, ocean temperature, the effect on the Earth of fires, solar radiation, thermal emission levels and a host of other data," all helping the scientific community delve into factors influencing our physical environment.[10] The satellite was launched into space in December 1999 aboard a Lockheed Martin Atlas IIAS, and between January and April 2002, Terra captured a series of images showing the retreat of the Larsen B ice shelf.

Lockheed Martin's array of weather satellites allows meteorologists to keep a steady watch on weather systems around the planet. And an increasingly sophisticated communications network and GPS have become essential tools for everything from the family road trip to advanced military operations.

GOES-R
The Geostationary Operational Environmental Satellite, first launched in 1975, has become integral to monitoring the world's weather. GOES, a geosynchronous satellite system, remains in orbit over the same location throughout its lifetime. GOES-1 took photographs of Earth, sending back images of weather that would have been otherwise impossible to predict and prepare for, providing early warning of severe weather systems such as hurricanes and thunderstorms. GOES-1 was retired in 1985, but the GOES series has continued to evolve.

The next generation of weather satellites developed by Lockheed Martin, GOES-R, will provide even better capability to support weather forecasters and the National Weather Service. Powerful new instruments on GOES-R include more visible and infrared channels, four times the imaging resolution and new lightning detection abilities. The Solar-Ultra-Violet Imager will monitor solar activity in ultraviolet wavelengths, providing key information on the effects of the sun on the Earth and near-Earth space environment. The Geostationary Lightning Mapper is a near-infrared instrument that maps total lightning (cloud-to-cloud and cloud-to-ground) over the Americas and adjacent oceans to provide improved tornado warning lead time and early indication of storm intensification and severe weather.

Thruster systems allow A2100s to maneuver into a geosynchronous position, making it possible and cost-effective to launch them in pairs.

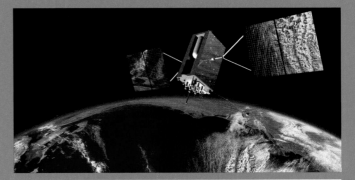

When the new constellation of GPS III satellites replaces the current generation's aging units in orbit, they will be more accurate, more powerful and more difficult for potential adversaries to jam. The satellites will provide enhanced positioning, navigation and timing services for both civilian and military users.

A2100

Lockheed Martin has designed, built and delivered over 100 commercial geostationary communications satellites to operators around the globe.

The A2100, Lockheed Martin's latest satellite platform, is highly modular and "catalogued to order," meaning customers do not have to pay for re-engineering or modifications to meet unique needs. Each satellite is built from a standard suite of components that can support multiple designs and functions. A2100 satellite platforms have been configured for commercial telecommunications use as well as for governmental use, such as the next generation of GOES-R weather satellites, Advanced Extremely High Frequency government communications satellites, the Mobile User Objective System and the new Global Positioning System satellites. Thruster systems allow A2100s to maneuver into a geosynchronous position, making it possible and cost-effective to launch them in pairs.

GPS III

In 2012, following the outstanding performance of its Global Positioning System IIR and IIR-M satellites, which are still orbiting today, Lockheed Martin continued work on the development and production of the first space vehicle for the next generation of GPS, known as GPS III, which will be delivered "flight ready" to the U.S. Air Force in 2014. Soon, GPS III satellites will have a signal that is three times stronger and eight times tougher to jam. The new satellites will have an expected operational life span of 15 years, about 25 percent longer than current orbiting GPS systems.

With GPS III's additional power and the new L1C signal, which makes it compatible with other international navigation satellites — such as the European Union's Galileo system and Russia's GLONASS — signal reception will improve in dense foliage and poor weather, as well as in rural canyons and congested cityscapes. Lockheed Martin is already working on a modification that will allow future GPS III satellites to be "dual launched" — two at a time on the same rocket booster — potentially saving the U.S. Air Force about $50 million per satellite in launch costs.

"THERE'S A CERTAIN FEELING OF COURAGE AND HOPE. YOU INSTINCTIVELY LOOK UP, NOT DOWN. YOU LOOK AHEAD, NOT BACK. YOU LOOK AHEAD WHERE THE HORIZONS ARE ABSOLUTELY UNLIMITED."[11]

—ROBERT GROSS, LOCKHEED CEO, 1957

VOYAGING TO OTHER WORLDS

While Lockheed Martin's satellites allowed humanity to understand our own world like never before, exploring space remained a priority in the first decade of the new millennium. For all intrepid voyagers and visionaries, the infinite frontier of space contains the potential for colonizing new worlds while better protecting our own.

With a new decade came a new cornerstone launch vehicle. The Atlas series of rockets, which carried the first American satellite into space in 1958 and the first American to orbit Earth in 1962, continued to evolve. The Atlas V is one of Lockheed Martin's vital contributions to the U.S. Air Force's Evolved Expendable Launch Vehicle program and America's access to space.

But the future of spacelift could lie in reusability. Lockheed Martin continues to investigate and demonstrate innovative technologies designed to produce both expendable and reusable launch systems that could save money and operate more efficiently.

Lockheed Martin is also designing the Origins-Spectral Interpretation-Resource Identification-Security-Regolith Explorer, or OSIRIS-REx spacecraft, which will launch in 2016, rendezvous with asteroid Bennu, and ultimately bring back samples to Earth. The samples will be the first of their kind for a U.S. mission and will reveal clues to the origin of our solar system and likely organic molecules that may have seeded life on Earth.

A United Launch Alliance Atlas V rocket launches the ICO G1 communication satellite, April 14, 2008. The first flight for many of these spacecraft actually came in the cargo hold of a Lockheed Martin C-5 Galaxy transport as they were being transported to launch sites.

Mars remains the next frontier of exploration. Lockheed Martin has designed and built nearly every capsule flown by NASA for space exploration since Apollo, but none as large as the Mars Science Laboratory aeroshell.

In 2008, the Lockheed Martin-built Phoenix Mars Lander exposed ice just below the planet's surface, confirming the existence of water on Mars.

AN EYE ON MARS

In 2002, the Mars Odyssey mission discovered huge deposits of hydrogen near the northern polar region of Mars, reigniting our fascination with the red planet and the possibility of water and the potential for life, past or present, on Mars. Odyssey also became the primary means of communication between NASA and the various Mars rovers exploring the planet's surface. Odyssey was so successful that its mission has been extended four times and continued into 2013.

Mars exploration focused on following water. In 2006, the Mars Reconnaissance Orbiter produced high-resolution images and helped determine the landing site for NASA's Phoenix Mars Lander, designed and built by Lockheed Martin. In 2008, the Phoenix's arrival in the Green Valley region of the Arctic Circle exposed ice on the planet's surface, finally confirming that there was water on Mars.

Just as the race to the moon defined space exploration of the 20th century, a human mission to Mars will be the crowning achievement of space exploration in the 21st century.

HUMAN SPACEFLIGHT

While robotic probes and rovers explored the red planet, the U.S. human spaceflight program experienced significant ups and downs during the 2000s. Astronauts logged the 100th spacewalk in the history of the U.S. space program in February 2001, and for a moment, it appeared that space travel might soon become commonplace.

The course of human spaceflight changed on February 1, 2003, when the Columbia space shuttle broke apart during re-entry, resulting in the tragic death of its seven crew members. The disaster, the first after a 14-year string of successful shuttle missions since return to flight following the Challenger tragedy in 1986, pointed to the continuing dangers of human spaceflight. Shuttle flights were grounded until 2005, when Discovery lifted off with seven crew members aboard, successfully returning to Earth, thus returning the shuttle program to flight status. An additional 21 successful shuttle missions were flown, closing an era of human spaceflight with the shuttle's final flight and safe return to Earth in July 2011.

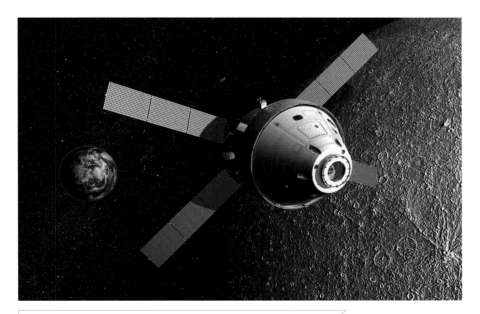

Artist's rendering of NASA's Orion Multi-Purpose Crew Vehicle, the future of human space exploration, designed and built by Lockheed Martin.

NASA Administrator Charlie Bolden and Lockheed Martin CEO and President Marillyn Hewson, who took the helm Jan. 1, 2013, signed a NASA Space Act Agreement to support strategic alliance for education and public outreach activities. The Exploration Design Challenge, targeted at grades K-12, will involve students in the flight test of their Orion spacecraft as part of this STEM (Science, Technology, Engineering and Math) initiative.

As one era ended, another began. NASA and Lockheed Martin are currently hard at work on Orion, the next generation of human spaceflight that will take astronauts to the moon, Mars, asteroids and other destinations in space. Designed to carry a crew of up to six, Orion looks more like the Apollo spacecraft than recent space shuttles. But there are major differences "under the hood." Though the Apollo program was one of the premier achievements of humankind, the technology used to run the spacecraft had less computing power than today's cellphones.

Orion is state of the art, incorporating the latest advances in computing, design, architecture and safety. Its systems are so evolved that even if every astronaut leaves the craft as part of the mission, Orion will continue to function. Solar panels eliminate the need for heavy fuel tanks, making the craft more maneuverable than Apollo-era craft even though it is 30 percent larger. Orion's interior will be roomier than the Apollo capsules, and its ascent and re-entry procedures are being designed to be 10 times safer than those of the space shuttles.

Orion is being designed to travel well beyond the moon and transport astronauts to and from distant destinations such as asteroids, the moons of Mars, and even the red planet itself. But beyond that, Orion is being designed to perform missions that have not yet even been dreamed of.

UNLOCKING SPACE'S SECRETS

Despite the end of the space shuttle program, another of Lockheed Martin's most impressive innovations — the Hubble Space Telescope — continues its unprecedented voyage of discovery. Five servicing missions allowed for routine maintenance of Hubble's spacecraft systems, extending its operational life, as well as significant upgrades to its state-of-the-art scientific instruments. The space-based observatory completed its 100,000th orbit around Earth in 2008 and millionth observation in 2011.

For more than two decades, Hubble breakthroughs have uncovered and sometimes even solved cosmic mysteries of how the universe has evolved. Using Hubble, astronomers discovered a mysterious form of "dark energy" that has been accelerating the universe's expansion. Hubble has also helped pinpoint the age of the universe (13.8 billion years old), analyzed supernovas and the chemical composition of far-off planets, hunted black holes, and examined the birth process of new stars. Gorgeous and inspiring images have given humanity a glimpse of the infinite, exquisitely captured by Hubble's cameras in visible, ultraviolet and near infrared light.

Complementing the Hubble Space Telescope is the Spitzer Space Telescope, another space-based observatory, which views the universe exclusively in the infrared portion of the electromagnetic spectrum. Developed by Lockheed Martin and launched into orbit in August 2003, Spitzer is a cornerstone of NASA's Cosmic Origins Program, helping us answer the timeless cosmic questions: Where did we come from? And where are we going?

Today, we find ourselves at a turning point in human history. While the Roman god Janus stood at the threshold of past and future, old and new, Lockheed Martin's satellites and telescopes traversing space are much more than modern-day myths. They are the practical manifestation of impossible ideas. From the earliest Loughead and Martin aeroplanes to the rudimentary missiles and space systems endeavoring to simply get off the ground, Lockheed Martin's modern-day systems enrich our comprehension of the disparate parts of our world, and connect our world to a deeper understanding of worlds we can only imagine. Looking back at the Earth and out into the beyond, our most impossible visions are becoming reality.

The Sombrero Galaxy as seen in infrared by the Spitzer Space Telescope.

EPILOGUE

THE NEXT 100 YEARS

Today's Lockheed Martin was born a century ago in a church and a garage, founded by pioneers with little more than lofty dreams. These were individuals with unrelenting vision, driven to take on challenges many deemed impossible. Since these humble beginnings, the story of Lockheed Martin has always been the story of people constantly seeing beyond obstacles into the future, trusting that technology holds the key to helping humanity address its most pressing challenges.

In the 1910s and '20s, the Loughead brothers and Glenn L. Martin helped pioneer powered flight and usher in a golden age of aviation.

In the '30s and '40s, the burgeoning Lockheed and Martin companies answered the call to power the arsenal of democracy for the Allies in World War II.

In the '50s and '60s, the companies looked beyond the skies to the stars, designing the rockets and spacecraft that slipped the bonds of gravity and accelerated the space race.

In the '70s and '80s, with the simmering Cold War threatening to boil over, Lockheed and Martin delivered the technology for global deterrents and intelligence that helped keep the peace.

And in the '90s and 2000s, a united Lockheed Martin helped lead the information technology revolution that transformed global security, government services and space exploration.

As Lockheed Martin looks to its next century, a host of new and seemingly impossible challenges await. Global security is growing more complex than ever. Worldwide IT networks are powering unprecedented efficiency but also creating unprecedented dangers for cyber defenders. The promise of clean, abundant and renewable energy is waiting to be fulfilled. As populations grow and change, the delivery of efficient and affordable services, health care and infrastructure becomes increasingly urgent. And the far reaches of space still beckon our astronauts, holding untold secrets of the universe.

Some might deem these challenges impossible. But Lockheed Martin's engineers, scientists and innovators are already rolling up their sleeves.

And in this new century, the voyagers and visionaries of Lockheed Martin will continue to transform the impossible into the inevitable.

LOCKHEED MARTIN
We never forget who we're working for®

ACKNOWLEDGEMENTS

Produced by Lockheed Martin Corporate Communications, Jennifer M. Whitlow, Vice President.

This book is the result of an exemplary team effort, and we would like to thank everyone who played a role in bringing the century-long history of this Corporation to life.

We would like to thank Adam Nemett, the book's lead author, for researching and writing the stories of Lockheed Martin's history, and for tackling the daunting task of compressing a century of achievements big and small into a few hundred pages of text and photos.

We'd also like to thank the following Lockheed Martin employees and retirees who went above and beyond in helping to make this book possible: Bob Abernethy, Peter Adams, Patty Apostolakes, Kevin Barre, Mickey Clemons, Jim Gring, Eric Hehs, Shauna Hidlebaugh, Eric Katz, Doug Kerr, Matt Kramer, Marcia Malinowski, Vince Marafino, Roger Mason, Frank Menaker, Sherm Mullin, Stan Piet, Jeff Rhodes, Steve Robinson, Trudy Sibley and Molly Townsend.

A very special thanks also goes out to the subject-matter experts who provided important historical and technical detail that helped bring the stories in this book to life: Sam Araki, Charlie Croom, Chester Kennedy, Chandra McMahon and Lee Wiegand. Special thanks to the Glenn L. Martin Maryland Aviation Museum for its assistance with fact-checking, research and support.

We are also grateful to the publication's operational and creative team at The History Factory: Rick Beller, David Buck, Anthony Crews, Jason Dressel, Sara Eagin, Peter Gianopulos, Amanda Guilmain, Alden Hathaway, Matthew Jent, Scott McMurray, Michelle Shirey, Ashley Walters, Bruce Weindruch and Michelle Witt.

Finally, our thanks to ColorGraphics and Renaissance Promotions for their role in creating, producing and distributing this book to tens of thousands of members of the Lockheed Martin team.

These lists are not exhaustive, and we value the contributions of dozens more people who helped us capture the remarkable history of this corporation's first 100 years. In honor and respect for the millions of individuals developing and utilizing Lockheed Martin's capabilities — those in uniform, in the air, in space, working on the front lines or toiling behind the scenes — we sincerely hope we succeeded in rendering your story authentically, if not exhaustively.

IMAGE CREDITS

Unless noted here, all images are courtesy of Lockheed Martin.

132 U.S. Navy; **133** John F. Kennedy Library, National Archives and Records Administration [193926]; **136** National Reconnaissance Office; **138** U.S. Air Force, Art Collection; **139** National Museum of the U.S. Air Force; **141** Department of Defense, U.S. Navy, U.S. Navy National Museum of Naval Aviation.

CHAPTER 6
146 NASA; **147** NASA; **154** National Reconnaissance Office; **157** U.S. Air Force, National Museum of the U.S. Air Force; **164** Courtesy Ronald Reagan Library; **165** ©Cliff; **172** NASA and STScI (Space Telescope Science Institute); **173** J.J. Hester (Arizona State University) and NASA.

CHAPTER 7
174 Smithsonian Institution National Air and Space Museum; **177** U.S. Air Force; **182** U.S. Navy; **185** ALPERT NATHAN, GPO.12/02/1991; **187** Department of Defense, U.S. Army; **189** U.S. Navy, DefenseImagery.mil; **196** NASA; **199** Department of Defense.

CHAPTER 8
203 Department of Defense; **204** U.S. Air Force; **205** U.S. Air Force, DefenseImagery. mil, Department of Defense, U.S. Navy; **208** Department of Defense, Defense.gov; **210** ©Greg Hume; **212** Satellite images by GeoEye.

CHAPTER 9
226 U.S. Navy; **227** U.S. Navy; **231** Smithsonian Institution National Postal Museum, U.S. Navy; **234** NASA, Earth Observatory, background photo courtesy of the U.S. Navy; **235** background photo courtesy of the U.S. Marines; **243** NASA/JPL-Caltech and The Hubble Heritage Team (STScI/AURA).

NOTES

CHAPTER 1

[1] Harwood, William B. *Raise Heaven and Earth*. New York: Simon & Schuster, 1993. p. 34.

[2] Boyne, Walter J. *Beyond the Horizons*. New York: St. Martin's Press, 1998. p. 6.

[3] London, Sol. "100th Anniversary of Aviation Pioneer Allan Lockheed," in Gil Cefaratt. *Lockheed: The People Behind the Story*. Paducah, KY: Turner Publishing Company, 2002. p. 6.

[4] Jakab, Peter L. "The Wright Brothers: Flight in Literature." Smithsonian's National Air and Space Museum Home Page. http://airandspace.si.edu/wrightbrothers/age/1914/literature.cfm.

[5] Harwood, *Raise Heaven and Earth*, p. 41.

[6] Harwood, *Raise Heaven and Earth*, p. 55.

[7] Harwood, *Raise Heaven and Earth*, p. 76.

[8] Boyne, *Beyond the Horizons*, p. 12.

[9] Ibid.

[10] Ibid.

[11] Rasmussen, Cecilia. "Seemingly Fearless Aviation Pioneer Was a Mama's Boy at Heart." *Los Angeles Times*, 28 September 2003. http://articles.latimes.com/2003/sep/28/local/me-then28.

[12] *The Call*. San Francisco, 22 June 1913. p. 17.

[13] Harwood, *Raise Heaven and Earth*, p. 99.

[14] Harwood, *Raise Heaven and Earth*, p. 101.

[15] Boyne, *Beyond the Horizons*, p. 16.

CHAPTER 2

[1] Harwood, *Raise Heaven and Earth*, p. 128.

[2] Kessner, Thomas. *The Flight of the Century: Charles Lindbergh and the Rise of American Aviation*. New York: Oxford University Press, 2010. p. 30.

[3] Boyne, *Beyond the Horizons*, p. 21.

[4] Boyne, *Beyond the Horizons*, p. 28.

[5] *Of Men and Stars: A History of Lockheed Aircraft Corporation*. Burbank, CA: Lockheed Aircraft Corporation, 1957, p. 6.

[6] *Amelia Earhart*. Directed by Nancy W. Porter. Narrated by Kathy Bates. Shanachie, 1993. DVD.

[7] Ibid.

[8] "Factsheets: Martin B-10." National Museum of the USAF. http://www.nationalmuseum.af.mil/factsheets/factsheet.asp?id=340.

[9] Christen, Harvey. Interview by Lockheed Oral History Project. 4 Feb 1982.

[10] Boyne, *Beyond the Horizons*, p. 61.

[11] Chappellet, Cyril. Interview by Lockheed Oral History Project. Personal interview. 12 Feb 1982.

CHAPTER 3

[1] "Rosie the Riveter: Real Women Workers in World War II (Journeys and Crossings, Library of Congress Digital Reference Section)." Library of Congress Home. www.loc.gov/rr/program/journey/rosie.html.

[2] Johnson, Clarence L., and Maggie Smith. *Kelly: More than My Share of It All*. Washington, D.C.: Smithsonian Institution Press, 1985. p. 62.

[3] Boyne, *Beyond the Horizons*, p. 91.

[4] *Of Men and Stars: A History of Lockheed Aircraft Corporation*. Burbank, CA: Lockheed Aircraft Corporation, 1957. p. 7.

[5] "Widows Get Airplane Jobs," *Poughkeepsie New Yorker*, 27 Jan 1942. p. 5.

[6] Cefaratt, Gil. *Lockheed: The People Behind the Story*, p. 21.

[7] Harwood, *Raise Heaven and Earth*, p. 217.

CHAPTER 4

[1] Johnson and Smith, *Kelly: More than My Share of It All*, pp. 97-98.

[2] "Telegram, George Kennan to James Byrnes ["Long Telegram"], February 22, 1946. Harry S. Truman Administration File, Elsey Papers." Harry S. Truman Library and Museum. www.trumanlibrary.org/whistlestop/study_collections/coldwar/documents/index.php?documentdate=1946-02-22&documentid=6-6&studycollectionid=&pagenumber=1.

[3] Orwell, George. "You and the Atomic Bomb." *Tribune*, 19 Oct 1945. http://orwell.ru/library/articles/ABomb/english/e_abomb.

[4] Higham, Robin D. S., and John W. Keeler. "F-80 Shooting Star." In *Flying American Combat Aircraft: The Cold War*. Mechanicsburg, PA: Stackpole Books, 2005. p. 151.

[5] Johnson and Smith, *Kelly: More than My Share of It All*, p. 80.

[6] *Preliminary Design of an Experimental World-circling Spaceship*. Special anniversary edition, 2005 ed. Santa Monica, CA: RAND, 1946. p.2.

[7] Mindling, George and Robert Bolton. *US Air Force Tactical Missiles*, 2011. p. 65.

[8] Griswold, Wesley S. "Remember the B-36?" *Popular Science*. Sept. 1961. p. 101.

[9] Johnson and Smith, *Kelly: More than My Share of It All*, p. 107.

[10] Harwood, *Raise Heaven and Earth*, p. 269.

[11] Taubman, Philip. *Secret Empire: Eisenhower, the CIA, and the Hidden Story of America's Space Espionage*. New York: Simon & Schuster, 2003. p. 140.

[12] Johnson and Smith, *Kelly: More than My Share of It All*, p. 125.

[13] Jacobsen, *Area 51*, p. 82.

CHAPTER 5

[1] Boyne, *Beyond the Horizons*, pp. 295, 303.

[2] Boyne, *Beyond the Horizons*, p. 292.

[3] Kennedy, John F. "Annual Message to the Congress on the State of the Union." The American Presidency Project. www.presidency.ucsb.edu/ws/?pid=8045.

[4] Araki, Sam. Interviews by Matthew Kramer. Phone interviews. Jan-Feb 2013.

[5] Ibid.

[6] McFadden, Robert. "James D. Hodgson, Labor Secretary, Dies at 96." *The New York Times*. www.nytimes.com/2012/12/11/us/james-d-hodgson-labor-secretary-dies-at-96.html?_r=0.

[7] Boyne, *Beyond the Horizons*, p. 243.

[8] Boyne, *Beyond the Horizons*, pp. 243-44.

[9] Kennedy, John F. "Excerpt from an Address Before a Joint Session of Congress, 25 May 1961." John F. Kennedy Presidential Library & Museum. www.jfklibrary.org/Asset-Viewer/xzw1gaeeT-ES6khED14P1Iw.aspx.

[10] Johnson and Smith. *Kelly: More than My Share of It All*. p. 137.

[11] Col. Jim Wadkins as quoted in Rich, Ben R., and Leo Janos. *Skunk Works: A Personal Memoir of My Years at Lockheed*. Boston: Little, Brown, 1994. p. 242.

[12] Honegger, Barbara and USAF Lt. Col. (Ret.) Hank Brandli. "USAF, Navy Weathermen Saved Apollo 11 Astronauts from Disaster." *Aviation Week & Space Technology*, 13 Dec 2004, p. 78.

CHAPTER 6

[1] Space Telescope Science Institute. "Hubble Essentials." HubbleSite. http://hubblesite.org/the_telescope/hubble_essentials.

[2] Freedman, Wayne. "Hubble engineer watches Atlantis liftoff." ABC Local. http://abclocal.go.com/kgo/story?section=news/local/south_bay&id=6808016.

[3] Nixon, Richard. "Richard Nixon: Inaugural Address." The American Presidency Project. www.presidency.ucsb.edu/ws/?pid=1941.

[4] Rich, Ben R., and Leo Janos. *Skunk Works: A Personal Memoir of My Years at Lockheed*. Boston: Little, Brown, 1994.; Brothers, Alan. "Obituary: Ben Rich." *The Independent*. 09 Jan 1995. www.independent.co.uk/news/people/obituary-ben-rich-1567201.html.

[5] Ingells, Douglas J. *L-1011 TriStar and the Lockheed Story*. Aero Publishers, 1973. p. 226.

[6] Boyne, Walter J. *The Two O'Clock War: The 1973 Yom Kippur Conflict and the Airlift That Saved Israel*. New York: Thomas Dunne Books, 2002. p. 279.

[7] Haulman, Daniel L. "Vietnam Evacuation: Operation Frequent Wind." Air Force Historical Studies Office. www.afhso.af.mil/shared/media/document/AFD-120823-033.pdf.

[8] Lockheed Martin. "Missions to Mars." 100 Years of Accelerating Tomorrow. www.lockheedmartin.com/us/100years/stories/mars-missions.html.

[9] Ibid.

[10] Chaisson, Eric J. *The Hubble Wars: Astrophysics Meets Astropolitics in the Two-Billion-Dollar Struggle Over the Hubble Space Telescope*. New York: HarperCollins Publishers, 1994. p. 30.

[11] Abella, Alex. *Soldiers of Reason: The RAND Corporation and the Rise of the American Empire*. Orlando, FL: Houghton Mifflin Harcourt, 4 May 2009. p. 255.

[12] Wilford, John Noble. "Spacecraft Passes a Critical Test." *The New York Times*, 2 Oct 1990. www.nytimes.com/1990/10/02/science/spacecraft-passes-a-critical-test.html?pagewanted=all&src=pm.

CHAPTER 7

[1] Araki, Sam. Interview by Matthew Jent and Adam Nemett. Phone interview. 14 Dec 2012. p. 12.

[2] Bush, George H.W. "Remarks by President Bush, Aug 5 1990." Margaret Thatcher Foundation. http://www.margaretthatcher.org/document/110704.

[3] "Operation Desert Storm: Evaluation of the Air Campaign," Washington, D.C.: United States General Accounting Office, Report to the Ranking Minority Member, Committee on Commerce, House of Representatives, June 1997, p. 125.

[4] Bush, George H. W. "Remarks to Raytheon Missile Systems Plant Employees in Andover, Massachusetts." The American Presidency Project. www.presidency.ucsb.edu/ws/?pid=19308.

[5] "Stealth Technology." *Modern Marvels*. The History Channel. 1997. Television.

[6] Air Force Magazine, August 1991, p. 35.

[7] Shelsby, Ted. "How the Deal Was Done: The Lockheed-Martin Marietta Merger." *The Baltimore Sun*. 12 Mar 1995. http://articles.baltimoresun.com/1995-03-12/news/1995071023_1_augustine-martin-marietta-lockheed-martin-corp.

[8] Shelsby, Ted. "Lockheed, Intel to make 3-D board graphics unit tailored for home, games use." *The Baltimore Sun*. http://articles.baltimoresun.com/1996-05-15/business/1996136096_1_computer-graphics-lockheed-martin-real-3-d.

[9] "Presidential Decision Directive NSTC-6." 28 March 1996. http://www.fas.org/spp/military/docops/national/gps.htm.

CHAPTER 8

[1] Bush, George W. "Address to Joint Session of Congress." Selected Speeches of President George W. Bush 2001-2008. http://georgewbush-whitehouse.archives.gov/infocus/bushrecord/documents/Selected_Speeches_George_W_Bush.pdf.

[2] Yenne, Bill. *Attack of the Drones, A History of Unmanned Aerial Combat*. St. Paul, MN: Zenith Imprint, 2004. p. 103.

[3] Press Release. "Desert Hawk Comes Up Big for British Army." Lockheed Martin. www.lockheedmartin.com/us/mst/eatures/110630-desert-hawk-comes-up-big-for-british-army-html.

[4] Gilmore, Gerry J. "Rumsfeld: Afghan, Iraq War Success Validates Budget Request." American Forces Press Service. U.S. Department of Defense. 15 May 2003. www.defense.gov/News/NewsArticle.aspx?ID=28981.

[5] "U.S. Army, Lockheed Martin Highlight M-TADS/PNVS Performance as Production Reaches 1,000 Systems." Reuters.com. http://www.reuters.com/article/2011/02/16/.idUS167281+16-Feb-2011+PRN20110216.

[6] "Rise of the Drones." *Nova*. Public Broadcasting Service. 2013. Television.

[7] "Factsheets: F-22 Raptor." National Museum of the USAF. http://www.af.mil/information/factsheets/factsheet.asp?id=199.

[8] "Collier Trophy 2000-2009 Award Winners." National Aeronautic Association. http://naa.aero/html/awards/index.cfm?cmsid=149.

[9] "Product Lines at Supship Bath." NAVSEA Supervisor of Shipbuilding, Conversion & Repair. www.navsea.navy.mil/supship/Bath/Products.aspx.

[10] Early, Ed. "Multiple Drug Seizures Highlight Freedom's 4th Fleet Deployment." U.S. Navy. 5 Apr 2010. www.public.navy.mil/surfor/lcs1/Pages/.MultipleDrugSeizuresHighlightFreedom's4thFleetDeployment.aspx.

[11] Cable News Network. "Lockheed Martin Wins Joint Strike Fighter Contract." CNN.com. http://transcripts.cnn.com/TRANSCRIPTS/0110/26/se.09.html.

CHAPTER 9

[1] Stevens, Robert J. "Remarks at the Paris Air Show Media Dinner, Le Bourget, France." Lockheed Martin. www.lockheedmartin.com/us/news/speeches/global-partners-building-global-security.html.

[2] Wiegand, Lee. Interview by Scott McMurray. Phone interview. 20 July 2012.

[3] Kennedy, Chester. Interview by Peter Gianopulos. Phone interview. 21 May 2012.

[4] "Inside Lockheed Martin's Human Immersive Lab: VR and Motion Tracking Solve F-35 Engineering Challenges." Motion Analysis from SME, Aerospace & Defense Manufacturing, 2010. www.motionanalysis.com/html/temp/lockheedHIL.html.

[5] "Immersive Simulation for Marine Corps Small Unit Training," Naval Research Advisory Committee. September 2009. p. 61. www.nrac.navy.mil/docs/2009_rpt_Immersive_Sim.pdf.

[6] Croom, Charles. Interview by Peter Gianopulos. Phone interview. 20 Nov 2012.

[7] McMahon, Chandra. Interview by Peter Gianopulos. Phone interview. 5 Dec 2012.

[8] Press Release. "Lockheed Martin Awarded $45 Million U.S. Postal Service Contract Modification." Lockheed Martin. www.lockheedmartin.com/us/news/press-releases/1998/september/LockheedMartinAwarded45MillionUSPos.html.

[9] McMahon, Chandra. Interview by Peter Gianopulos. Phone interview. 5 Dec 2012.

[10] Di Nardo, Tom. "An Era Ends In King Of Prussia: Lockheed Martin's Last Satellite Flies." *Daily News*. http://articles.philly.com/1999-04-15/business/25519101_1_atlas-rocket-nasa-s-terra-spacecraft.

[11] Cefaratt, Gil, and Jack G. Real. "Birth of the C-130 (Hercules)." In *Lockheed: The People Behind the Story*. Limited ed. Paducah, KY: Turner Publishing Company, 2002. p. 70.

SELECTED BIBLIOGRAPHY

A Century of Flight: 100 Years of Aviation. DVD. Directed by Edward Feuerherd. Chatsworth, CA: Distributed by Image/Madacy Home Video, 2004.

Abella, Alex. *Soldiers of Reason: The RAND Corporation and the Rise of the American Empire*. Orlando, FL: Harcourt, Inc., 2008.

Amelia Earhart. DVD. Directed by Nancy W. Porter. Boston: Shanachie, 1993.

America's Hangar. DVD. Directed by Gary Wortman. United States: Smithsonian Networks, 2007.

Berg, A. Scott. *Lindbergh*. New York: Putnam, 1998.

Boyne, Walter J. *Beyond the Horizons: The Lockheed Story*. New York: Thomas Dunne Books, 1998.

Boyne, Walter J. *The Two O'clock War: The 1973 Yom Kippur Conflict and the Airlift That Saved Israel*. New York: Thomas Dunne Books, 2002.

Breihan, John R., and Stan Piet. *Martin Aircraft, 1909-1960*. Santa Ana, CA: Narkiewicz/Thompson, 1995.

Bright, Charles D. *The Jet Makers: The Aerospace Industry from 1945 to 1972*. Lawrence, KS: Regents Press of Kansas, 1978.

Cable News Network. "Lockheed Martin Wins Joint Strike Fighter Contract." CNN. com. http://transcripts.cnn.com/TRANSCRIPTS/0110/26/se.09.html.

Cadbury, Deborah. *Space Race: The Epic Battle Between America and the Soviet Union for Dominion of Space*. New York: HarperCollins, 2006.

Cefaratt, Gil. *Lockheed: The People Behind the Story*. Limited Ed. Paducah, KY: Turner Publications, 2002.

Chaisson, Eric. *The Hubble Wars: Astrophysics Meets Astropolitics in the Two-Billion-Dollar Struggle Over the Hubble Space Telescope.* New York: HarperCollins, 1994.

Cheatham, Mike. *No Man Walks Alone: The Life and Times of Thomas G. Pownall.* Macon, GA: Mercer University Press, 2003.

Colman, Penny. *Rosie the Riveter: Women Working on the Home Front in World War II.* New York: Crown Publishers, 1995.

Crouch, Tom D. *Wings: A History of Aviation From Kites to the Space Age.* Washington, D.C.: Smithsonian National Air and Space Museum, 2003.

Press Release. "Desert Hawk Comes Up Big for British Army." Lockheed Martin. www.lockheedmartin.com/us/mst/features/110630-desert-hawk-comes-up-big-for-british-army-.html.

Dick, Steven J. *America in Space: NASA's First Fifty Years.* New York: Abrams, 2007.

Early, Ed. "Multiple Drug Seizures Highlight Freedom's 4th Fleet Deployment." U.S. Navy. www.public.navy.mil/surfor/lcs1/Pages/MultipleDrugSeizuresHighlightFreedom's4thFleetDeployment.aspx.

Eden, Paul, and Soph Moeng. *The Complete Encyclopedia of World Aircraft.* New York: Barnes & Noble Books, 2002.

"Factsheets: Consolidated PT-1 Trusty." National Museum of the USAF. www.nationalmuseum.af.mil/factsheets/factsheet.asp?id=333.

Fitzsimons, Bernard. *The Illustrated Encyclopedia of 20th Century Weapons and Warfare.* Milwaukee: Purnell Reference Books, 1979.

Freedman, Wayne. "Hubble engineer watches Atlantis liftoff." ABC Local. http://abclocal.go.com/kgo/story?section=news/local/south_bay&id=6808016.

Gilmore, Gerry J. "Rumsfeld: Afghan, Iraq War Success Validates Budget Request." United States Department of Defense. www.defense.gov/News/NewsArticle. aspx?ID=28981.

Goddard, Seth. "Life Hero of the Week Profile." Amelia Earhart: First Lady of the Sky. www.life.com.

Grant, R. G. *Flight: 100 Years of Aviation*. New York: DK Publishing, 2002.

Halpin, James F. *Zero Defects: A New Dimension in Quality Assurance*. New York: McGraw-Hill, 1966.

Harley, Ruth W., and Robert Doremus. *Glenn L. Martin: Boy Conqueror of the Air*. Indianapolis: Bobbs-Merrill, 1967.

Harwood, William B. *Raise Heaven and Earth: The Story of Martin Marietta People and Their Pioneering Achievements*. New York: Simon & Schuster, 1993.

Haulman, Daniel L. "Vietnam Evacuation: Operation Frequent Wind." Air Force Historical Studies Office. www.afhso.af.mil/shared/media/document/ AFD-120823-033.pdf.

Higham, Robin D. S., and John W. Keeler. "F-80 Shooting Star." In *Flying American Combat Aircraft: The Cold War*. Mechanicsburg, PA: Stackpole Books, 2005.

Honegger, Barbara and USAF Lt. Col. (Ret.) Hank Brandli. "USAF, Navy Weathermen Saved Apollo 11 Astronauts from Disaster." *Aviation Week & Space Technology*, 13 Dec 2004.

Space Telescope Science Institute. "Hubble Essentials." HubbleSite. http:// hubblesite.org/the_telescope/hubble_essentials/.

"Immersive Simulation for Marine Corps Small Unit Training." Naval Research Advisory Committee. www.nrac.navy.mil/.

"Inside Lockheed's Human Immersive Lab: VR and Motion Tracking Solve F-35 Engineering Challenges." Motion Analysis Corporation. www.motionanalysis.com/html/temp/lockheedHIL.html.

Jacobsen, Annie. *Area 51: An Uncensored History of America's Top Secret Military Base*. New York: Little, Brown and Co., 2011.

Jakab, Peter L. "The Wright Brothers: Flight in Literature." Smithsonian's National Air and Space Museum Home Page. http://airandspace.si.edu/wrightbrothers/age/1914/literature.cfm.

Johnson, Clarence L., and Maggie Smith. *Kelly: More Than My Share of It All*. Washington, D.C.: Smithsonian Institution Press, 1985.

Kennedy, John F. "Excerpt from an Address Before a Joint Session of Congress, 25 May 1961." John F. Kennedy Presidential Library & Museum. www.jfklibrary.org/Asset-Viewer/xzw1gaeeTES6khED14P1Iw.aspx.

Kennedy, John F. "John F. Kennedy: Annual Message to the Congress on the State of the Union." The American Presidency Project. www.presidency.ucsb.edu/ws/?pid=8045.

Kessner, Thomas. *The Flight of the Century: Charles Lindbergh & The Rise of American Aviation*. New York: Oxford University Press, 2010.

Lindbergh, Anne Morrow, and Charles A. Lindbergh. *North to the Orient*. New York: Harcourt, Brace and Co., 1935.

Press Release. "Lockheed Martin Awarded $45 Million U.S. Postal Service Contract Modification." Lockheed Martin. www.lockheedmartin.com/us/news/press-releases/1998/september/LockheedMartinAwarded45MillionUSPos.html.

Lovick, Edward. *Radar Man: A Personal History of Stealth*. New York: iUniverse, 2010.

McFadden, Robert. "James D. Hodgson, Labor Secretary, Dies at 96." *The New York Times*. www.nytimes.com/2012/12/11/us/james-d-hodgson-labor-secretary-dies-at-96.html?_r=0.

Mewhinney, Mike. "NASA - Kuiper Airborne Observatory Marks 30th Anniversary of its Dedication." NASA. www.nasa.gov/vision/universe/watchtheskies/kuiper.html.

Nixon, Richard. "Richard Nixon: Inaugural Address." The American Presidency Project. www.presidency.ucsb.edu/ws/?pid=1941.

Of Men and Stars: A History of Lockheed Aircraft Corporation. Burbank, CA: Lockheed Aircraft Corporation, 1957.

Operation Desert Storm: Evaluation of the Air War. Washington, D.C.: United States General Accounting Office, 1996.

Orwell, George. "You and the Atomic Bomb." George Orwell. http://orwell.ru/library/articles/ABomb/english/e_abomb.

Ottaviani, Jim, Zander Cannon, and Kevin Cannon. *T-Minus: The Race to the Moon*. New York: Aladdin, 2009.

Preliminary Design of an Experimental World-circling Spaceship. Special anniversary edition, 2005 ed. Santa Monica, CA: RAND, 1946.

"Product Lines at Supship Bath." NAVSEA Supervisor of Shipbuilding, Conversion & Repair. www.navsea.navy.mil/supship/Bath/Products.aspx.

Rasmussen, Cecilia. "Seemingly Fearless Aviation Pioneer Was a Mama's Boy at Heart." *Los Angeles Times*, 28 September 2003. http://articles.latimes.com/2003/sep/28/local/me-then28.

Rich, Ben R., and Leo Janos. *Skunk Works: A Personal Memoir of My Years at Lockheed*. Boston: Little, Brown, 1994.

"Rosie the Riveter: Real Women Workers in World War II." Journeys and Crossings, Library of Congress Digital Reference Section. Library of Congress. www.loc.gov/rr/program/journey/rosie.html.

Schefter, James L. *The Race: The Complete True Story of How America Beat Russia to the Moon*. New York: Anchor Books, 2000.

Shelsby, Ted. "Lockheed Martin Merger: How the Deal Was Done." *The Baltimore Sun*. http://articles.baltimoresun.com/1995-03-12/news/1995071023_1_augustine-martin-marietta-lockheed-martin-corp.

Shelsby, Ted. "Lockheed, Intel to Make 3-D Board Graphics Unit Tailored for Home Games Use." *The Baltimore Sun*. http://articles.baltimoresun.com/1996-05-15/business/1996136096_1_computer-graphics-lockheed-martin-real-3-d.

Stevens, Robert J. "Remarks at the Paris Air Show Media Dinner, Le Bourget, France." Lockheed Martin. www.lockheedmartin.com/us/news/speeches/global-partners-building-global-security.html.

Still, Henry. *To Ride the Wind: A Biography of Glenn L. Martin*. New York: Messner, 1964.

Sweetman, Bill, and James C. Goodall. *Lockheed F-117A: Operation and Development of the Stealth Fighter*. Osceola, WI: Motorbooks International, 1990.

Taubman, Philip. *Secret Empire: Eisenhower, the CIA, and the Hidden Story of America's Space Espionage*. New York: Simon & Schuster, 2003.

"Telegram, George Kennan to James Byrnes ["Long Telegram"], February 22, 1946. Harry S. Truman Administration File, Elsey Papers." Harry S. Truman Library and Museum. www.trumanlibrary.org/whistlestop/study_collections/coldwar/documents/index.php?documentdate=1946-02-22&documentid=6-6&studycollectionid=&pagenumber=1.

Wilford, John Noble. "Spacecraft Passes a Critical Test." *The New York Times*. www.nytimes.com/1990/10/02/science/spacecraft-passes-a-critical-test. html?pagewanted=all&src=pm.

Yenne, Bill. *Lockheed*. New York: Crescent Books, 1987.

Yoshino, Ronald W. *Lightning Strikes: The 475th Fighter Group in the Pacific War, 1943-1945*. Manhattan, KS: Sunflower University Press, 1988.

INDEX